EMMA

Jane Austen

INTRODUCTION:
STOPPING TO BUY SPARKNOTES ON A SNOWY EVENING

Whose words these are you *think* you know.
Your paper's due tomorrow, though;
We're glad to see you stopping here
To get some help before you go.

Lost your course? You'll find it here.
Face tests and essays without fear.
Between the words, good grades at stake:
Get great results throughout the year.

Once school bells caused your heart to quake
As teachers circled each mistake.
Use SparkNotes and no longer weep,
Ace every single test you take.

Yes, books are lovely, dark, and deep,
But only what you grasp you keep,
With hours to go before you sleep,
With hours to go before you sleep.

CONTENTS

CONTEXT

Jane Austen, whom some critics consider England's best novelist, was born in 1775 in Steventon, England. The seventh of eight children, Austen lived with her parents for her entire life, first in Steventon and later in Bath, Southampton, and Chawton. Her father was the parish rector in Steventon, and, though not wealthy, her family was well connected and well educated. Austen briefly attended boarding school in Reading but received the majority of her education at home. According to rumor, she had a brief love affair when she was twenty-five, but it did not lead to a marriage proposal. Two years later she accepted and then quickly rejected a proposal. She remained unmarried for the rest of her life. Austen died in 1817, at age forty-one, of Addison's disease.

Austen began writing stories at a very young age and completed her first novel in her early twenties. However, she did not publish until 1811, when *Sense and Sensibility* appeared anonymously, followed by *Pride and Prejudice* (1813) and *Mansfield Park* (1814). *Emma,* which appeared in 1816, was the last novel published during Austen's lifetime. (*Northanger Abbey* and *Persuasion* appeared posthumously.)

Austen's novels received little critical or popular recognition during her lifetime, and her identity as a novelist was not revealed until after her death. As admired as Austen's novels later became, critics have had a difficult time placing them within literary history. She is known for her gently satirical portraits of village life and of the rituals of courtship and marriage, but she wrote during the Romantic period, when most major writers were concerned with a very different set of interests and values. Romantic poets confronted the hopes and failures of the French Revolution and formulated new literary values centered on individual freedom, passion, and intensity. In comparison, Austen's detailed examination of the rules of decorum that govern social relationships, and her insistence that reason and moderation are necessary checks on feeling, make her seem out of step with the literary times. One way to understand Austen's place in literary history is to think of her as part of the earlier eighteenth century, the Age of Reason, when literature was associated with wit, poise, and propriety. Her novels certainly belong to an eighteenth-century genre, the comedy of manners, which examines the behavior of men and women of a single social class.

Rather than dismiss Austen as a writer who shuns the artistic and political movements of her time, it is perhaps more useful to think of her as an early feminist. Critics have pointed out that the Romantics, who were almost exclusively male, offered a poor model of literary fulfillment for the ambitious woman of the time. While male writers such as Percy Bysshe Shelley and Lord Byron possessed the freedom to promote their own individuality through wide travel and sexual and military adventurism, women were largely denied these freedoms. For women, the penalty for sexual freedom was social ostracism, poverty, and worse. In *Sense and Sensibility,* Austen describes explicitly the danger that cultivating emotion posed for women of her time.

In this social context, Austen's commitment to reason and moderation can be seen as feminist and progressive rather than conservative. The intelligence and resourcefulness of her heroines stand in constant contrast to the limits of the constricted world of courtship and marriage defining their sphere of action. While reading *Emma* it is interesting to consider to what extent Austen accepts or questions the idea that marriage represents a woman's maturity and fulfillment.

Some consider *Emma* Austen's best and most representative novel. It is also her longest novel, and by many accounts, her most difficult. Long praised for its rich domestic realism, *Emma* also presents puzzling questions: how can a character as intelligent as Emma be wrong so often? When does Austen expect us to sympathize with Emma, and when does she expect us to criticize her? Is the ending as genuinely happy as it is presented to be, or does Austen subtly inject a note of subversive irony into it? That these questions are on some level unanswerable ensures that *Emma* will be read again and again.

Plot Overview

A LTHOUGH CONVINCED that she herself will never marry, Emma Woodhouse, a precocious twenty-year-old resident of the village of Highbury, imagines herself to be naturally gifted in conjuring love matches. After self-declared success at matchmaking between her governess and Mr. Weston, a village widower, Emma takes it upon herself to find an eligible match for her new friend, Harriet Smith. Though Harriet's parentage is unknown, Emma is convinced that Harriet deserves to be a gentleman's wife and sets her friend's sights on Mr. Elton, the village vicar. Meanwhile, Emma persuades Harriet to reject the proposal of Robert Martin, a well-to-do farmer for whom Harriet clearly has feelings.

Harriet becomes infatuated with Mr. Elton under Emma's encouragement, but Emma's plans go awry when Elton makes it clear that his affection is for Emma, not Harriet. Emma realizes that her obsession with making a match for Harriet has blinded her to the true nature of the situation. Mr. Knightley, Emma's brother-in-law and treasured friend, watches Emma's matchmaking efforts with a critical eye. He believes that Mr. Martin is a worthy young man whom Harriet would be lucky to marry. He and Emma quarrel over Emma's meddling, and, as usual, Mr. Knightley proves to be the wiser of the pair. Elton, spurned by Emma and offended by her insinuation that Harriet is his equal, leaves for the town of Bath and marries a girl there almost immediately.

Emma is left to comfort Harriet and to wonder about the character of a new visitor expected in Highbury—Mr. Weston's son, Frank Churchill. Frank is set to visit his father in Highbury after having been raised by his aunt and uncle in London, who have taken him as their heir. Emma knows nothing about Frank, who has long been deterred from visiting his father by his aunt's illnesses and complaints. Mr. Knightley is immediately suspicious of the young man, especially after Frank rushes back to London merely to have his hair cut. Emma, however, finds Frank delightful and notices that his charms are directed mainly toward her. Though she plans to discourage these charms, she finds herself flattered and engaged in a flirtation with the young man. Emma greets Jane Fairfax, another addition to the Highbury set, with less enthusiasm. Jane is beautiful and accomplished, but Emma dislikes her because of her reserve and, the narrator insinuates, because she is jealous of Jane.

Suspicion, intrigue, and misunderstandings ensue. Mr. Knightley defends Jane, saying that she deserves compassion because, unlike Emma, she has no independent fortune and must soon leave home to work as a governess. Mrs. Weston suspects that the warmth of Mr. Knightley's defense comes from romantic feelings, an implication Emma resists. Everyone assumes that Frank and Emma are forming an attachment, though Emma soon dismisses Frank as a potential suitor and imagines him as a match for Harriet. At a village ball, Knightley earns Emma's approval by offering to dance with Harriet, who has just been humiliated by Mr. Elton and his new wife. The next day, Frank saves Harriet from Gypsy beggars. When Harriet tells Emma that she has fallen in love with a man above her social station, Emma believes that she means Frank. Knightley begins to suspect that Frank and Jane have a secret understanding, and he attempts to warn Emma. Emma laughs at Knightley's suggestion and loses Knightley's approval when she flirts with Frank and insults Miss Bates, a kindhearted spinster and Jane's aunt, at a picnic. When Knightley reprimands Emma, she weeps.

News comes that Frank's aunt has died, and this event paves the way for an unexpected revelation that slowly solves the mysteries. Frank and Jane have been secretly engaged; his attentions to Emma have been a screen to hide his true preference. With his aunt's death and his uncle's approval, Frank can now marry Jane, the woman he loves. Emma worries that Harriet will be crushed, but she soon discovers that it is Knightley, not Frank, who is the object of Harriet's affection. Harriet believes that Knightley shares her feelings. Emma finds herself upset by Harriet's revelation, and her distress forces her to realize that she is in love with Knightley. Emma expects Knightley to tell her he loves Harriet, but, to her delight, Knightley declares his love for Emma. Harriet is soon comforted by a second proposal from Robert Martin, which she accepts. The novel ends with the marriage of Harriet and Mr. Martin and that of Emma and Mr. Knightley, resolving the question of who loves whom after all.

CHARACTER LIST

Emma Woodhouse The protagonist of the novel. In the well-known first sentence of the novel, the narrator describes Emma as "handsome, clever, and rich, with a comfortable home and happy disposition." In some ways, the twenty-year-old Emma is mature for her age. Because her mother is dead and her older sister married, she is already the head of her father's household. She cares for her father and oversees the social goings-on in the village of Highbury. Emma's misplaced confidence in her abilities as a matchmaker and her prudish fear of love constitute the central focus of the novel, which traces Emma's mistakes and growing self-understanding.

Mr. George Knightley Emma's brother-in-law and the Woodhouses' trusted friend and advisor. Knightley is a respected landowner in his late thirties. He lives at Donwell Abbey and leases property to the Martins, a family of wealthy farmers whom he likes and counsels. Knightley is the only character who is openly critical of Emma, pointing out her flaws and foibles with frankness, out of genuine concern and care for her. In this respect, he acts as a stand-in for Austen's and the reader's judgments of Emma.

Mr. Woodhouse Emma's father and the patriarch of Hartfield, the Woodhouse estate. Though Mr. Woodhouse is nervous, frail, and prone to hypochondria, he is also known for his friendliness and his attachment to his daughter. He is very resistant to change, to the point that he is unhappy to see his daughters or Emma's governess marry. In this sense, he impedes Emma's growth and acceptance of her adult destiny. He is often foolish and clearly not Emma's intellectual equal, but she comforts and entertains him with insight and affection.

Harriet Smith   A pretty but unremarkable seventeen-year-old woman of uncertain parentage, who lives at the local boarding school. Harriet becomes Emma's protégé and the object of her matchmaking schemes.

Frank Churchill   Mr. Weston's son and Mrs. Weston's stepson. Frank Churchill lives at Enscombe with his aunt and uncle, Mr. and Mrs. Churchill. He is considered a potential suitor for Emma, but she learns that though Frank is attractive, charming, and clever, he is also irresponsible, deceitful, rash, and ultimately unsuited to her.

Jane Fairfax   Miss Bates's niece, whose arrival in Highbury irritates Emma. Jane rivals Emma in accomplishment and beauty; she possesses a kind heart and a reserved temperament. Because Jane lacks Emma's fortune, she must consider employment as a governess, but her marriage to Frank Churchill saves her from that fate.

Mrs. Weston   Formerly Miss Taylor, Emma's beloved governess and companion. Known for her kind temperament and her devotion to Emma, Mrs. Weston lives at Randalls with her husband, Frank Churchill's father.

Mr. Weston   The widower and proprietor of Randalls, who has just married Miss Taylor when the novel begins. Mr. Weston has a son, Frank, from his first marriage to Miss Churchill (Frank was raised by Miss Churchill's sister and brother-in-law). Mr. Weston is warm, sociable, and perpetually optimistic.

Mr. Elton   The village vicar, a handsome and agreeable man considered a welcome addition to any social gathering. When he reveals his indifference to Harriet and his desire to marry Emma, only to take a bride at Bath shortly thereafter, he comes to seem proud, conceited, and superficial.

Mr. Robert Martin A twenty-four-year-old farmer. Mr. Martin is industrious and good-hearted, though he lacks the refinements of a gentleman. He lives at Abbey-Mill Farm, a property owned by Knightley, with his mother and sisters.

Miss Bates Friend of Mr. Woodhouse and aunt of Jane Fairfax, Miss Bates is a middle-aged spinster without beauty or cleverness but with universal goodwill and a gentle temperament. Emma's impatient treatment of her reveals the less attractive parts of Emma's character.

Isabella Knightley Emma's older sister, who lives in London with her husband, Mr. John Knightley, and their five children. Isabella is pretty, amiable, and completely devoted to her family, but slow and diffident compared to Emma. Her domesticity provides a contrast to the independent celibacy Emma imagines for herself.

Mr. John Knightley Emma's brother-in-law, and Mr. George Knightley's brother. As a lawyer, John Knightley is clear-minded but somewhat sharp in temper, and Emma and her father are sometimes displeased with his severity.

Mrs. Elton Formerly Augusta Hawkins, Mrs. Elton hails from Bristol and meets Mr. Elton in Bath. She is somewhat attractive and accomplished; she has some fortune and a well-married sister, but her vanity, superficiality, and vulgar overfamiliarity offset her admirable qualities.

Mrs. Churchill Mr. Weston's ailing former sister-in-law and Frank Churchill's aunt and guardian. She is known to be capricious, ill-tempered, and extremely possessive of Frank. Frank is able to marry Jane Fairfax, as he desires, only after Mrs. Churchill's death.

Colonel Campbell A friend of Jane Fairfax's father who lives in London and who takes charge of orphaned Jane when she is eight years old. Colonel Campbell feels great affection for Jane but is unable to provide her with an inheritance.

Mrs. Dixon The Campbells' daughter and Jane's friend. Mrs. Dixon lacks beauty and lives with her husband in Ireland.

Mr. Dixon Husband to the Campbells' daughter. Emma suspects that Mr. Dixon had a romance with Jane Fairfax before his marriage.

Mrs. Goddard Mistress of the local boarding school. Mrs. Goddard introduces Harriet Smith to the Woodhouses.

Mrs. Bates Mother to Miss Bates and friend of Mr. Woodhouse. An elderly woman, Mrs. Bates is quiet, amiable, and somewhat deaf.

Mr. Perry An apothecary and associate of Emma's father. Mr. Perry is highly esteemed by Mr. Woodhouse for his medical advice even though he is not a proper physician, and Mr. Woodhouse argues with his daughter Isabella over Perry's recommendations.

Elizabeth Martin Mr. Martin's kind sister, with whom Harriet was good friends before meeting Emma and turning down Mr. Martin's marriage proposal. Harriet's feelings of guilt and her desire to rekindle her relationship with Elizabeth pose a dilemma for Emma, who finds the Martins pleasant, worthy people, but worries that Harriet may be tempted to accept Mr. Martin's offer if she again grows close with the family.

Mr. and Mrs. Cole Tradespeople and longtime residents of Highbury whose good fortune of the past several years has led them to adopt a luxurious lifestyle that is only a notch below that of the Woodhouses. Offended by their attempt to transcend their "only moderately genteel" social status, Emma has long been preparing to turn down any dinner invitation from the Coles in order to teach them their folly in thinking they can interact socially with the likes of her family. Like the Martins, the Coles are the means through which Emma demonstrates her class-consciousness.

ANALYSIS OF MAJOR CHARACTERS

EMMA WOODHOUSE

The narrator introduces Emma to us by emphasizing her good fortune: "handsome, clever, and rich, with a comfortable home and happy disposition," Emma "had lived nearly twenty-one years in the world with very little to distress or vex her." But, the narrator warns us, Emma possesses "the power of having rather too much her own way, and a disposition to think a little too well of herself." Emma's stubbornness and vanity produce many of the novel's conflicts, as Emma struggles to develop emotionally.

Emma makes three major mistakes. First, she attempts to make Harriet into the wife of a gentleman, when Harriet's social position dictates that she would be better suited to the farmer who loves her. Then, she flirts with Frank Churchill even though she does not care for him, making unfair comments about Jane Fairfax along the way. Most important, she does not realize that, rather than being committed to staying single (as she always claims), she is in love with and wants to marry Mr. Knightley. Though these mistakes seriously threaten Harriet's happiness, cause Emma embarrassment, and create obstacles to Emma's own achievement of true love, none of them has lasting consequences. Throughout the novel, Knightley corrects and guides Emma; in marrying Knightley, Emma signals that her judgment has aligned with his.

Austen predicted that Emma would be "a character whom no one but me will much like." Though most of Austen's readers have proven her wrong, her narration creates many ambiguities. The novel is narrated using free indirect discourse, which means that, although the all-knowing narrator speaks in the third person, she often relates things from Emma's point of view and describes things in language we might imagine Emma using. This style of narration creates a complex mixture of sympathy with Emma and ironic judgment on her behavior. It is not always clear when we are to share Emma's perceptions and when we are to see through them. Nor do we know how harshly Austen expects us to judge Emma's behavior.

Though this narrative strategy creates problems of interpretation for the reader, it makes Emma a richly multidimensional character.

Emma does not have one specific foil, but the implicit distinctions made between her and the other women in the novel offer us a context within which to evaluate her character. Jane is similar to Emma in most ways, but she does not have Emma's financial independence, so her difficulties underscore Emma's privileged nature. Mrs. Elton, like Emma, is independent and imposes her will upon her friends, but her crudeness and vanity reinforce our sense of Emma's refinement and fundamentally good heart. Emma's sister, Isabella, is stereo-typically feminine—soft-hearted, completely devoted to her family, dependent, and not terribly bright. The novel implicitly prefers Emma's independence and cleverness to her sister's more traditional deportment, although we are still faced with the paradox that though Emma is clever, she is almost always mistaken.

MR. KNIGHTLEY

Mr. Knightley serves as the novel's model of good sense. From his very first conversation with Emma and her father in Chapter 1, his purpose—to correct the excesses and missteps of those around him—is clear. He is unfailingly honest but tempers his honesty with tact and kindheartedness. Almost always, we can depend upon him to provide the correct evaluation of the other characters' behavior and personal worth. He intuitively understands and kindly makes allowances for Mr. Woodhouse's whims; he is sympathetic and protective of the women in the community, including Jane, Harriet, and Miss Bates; and, most of all, even though he frequently disapproves of her behavior, he dotes on Emma.

Knightley's love for Emma—the one emotion he cannot govern fully—leads to his only lapses of judgment and self-control. Before even meeting Frank, Knightley decides that he does not like him. It gradually becomes clear that Knightley feels jealous—he does not welcome a rival. When Knightley believes Emma has become too attached to Frank, he acts with uncharacteristic impulsiveness in running away to London. His declaration of love on his return bursts out uncontrollably, unlike most of his prudent, well-planned actions. Yet Knightley's loss of control humanizes him rather than making him seem like a failure.

Like Emma, Knightley stands out in comparison to his peers. His brother, Mr. John Knightley, shares his clear-sightedness but lacks his unfailing kindness and tact. Both Frank and Knightley are perceptive, warm-hearted, and dynamic; but whereas Frank uses his intelligence to conceal his real feelings and invent clever compliments to please those around him, Knightley uses his intelligence to discern right moral conduct. Knightley has little use for cleverness for its own sake; he rates propriety and concern for others more highly.

FRANK CHURCHILL

Frank epitomizes attractiveness in speech, manner, and appearance. He goes out of his way to please everyone, and, while the more perceptive characters question his seriousness, everyone except Knightley is charmed enough to be willing to indulge him. Frank is the character who most resembles Emma, a connection she points out at the novel's close when she states that "destiny ... connect[s] us with two characters so much superior to our own." Like Emma, Frank develops over the course of the novel by trading a somewhat vain and superficial perspective on the world for the seriousness brought on by the experience of genuine suffering and love. He is a complex character because though we know we should judge him harshly in moral terms, we cannot help but like him more than he deserves to be liked.

JANE FAIRFAX

Jane's beauty and accomplishment immediately make her stand out, but we are likely to follow Emma's lead at first and judge Jane uninteresting on account of her reserve. As Jane gradually betrays more personality and emotion, she indicates that she harbors some secret sorrow. Eventually, she and Emma push the cloudy confusion behind and become friends. The contrast between Jane's delicate sense of propriety and morality and the passionate nature of her feelings is much more dramatic than any of the conflicts that Emma experiences. Jane's situation too is much more dire than Emma's: if Jane does not wed, she must become a governess, because she lacks any money of her own. The revelation of Jane's secret engagement to Frank makes Jane seem more human, just as Knightley's humanity is brought out by his love for Emma.

THEMES, MOTIFS & SYMBOLS

THEMES

Themes are the fundamental and often universal ideas explored in a literary work.

MARRIAGE AND SOCIAL STATUS

Emma is structured around a number of marriages recently consummated or anticipated, and, in each case, the match solidifies the participant's social status. In Austen's time, social status was determined by a combination of family background, reputation, and wealth—marriage was one of the main ways in which one could raise one's social status. This method of social advancement was especially crucial to women, who were denied the possibility of improving their status through hard work or personal achievement.

Yet, the novel suggests, marrying too far above oneself leads to strife. Mr. Weston's first marriage to Miss Churchill had ostensibly been a good move for him, because she came from a wealthy and well-connected family (Mr. Weston is a tradesman), but the inequality of the relationship caused hardship to both. He marries Mrs. Weston just prior to the novel's opening, and this second marriage is happier because their social statuses are more equal—Mrs. Weston is a governess, and thus very fortunate to be rescued from her need to work by her marriage. Emma's attempt to match Harriet with Mr. Elton is also shunned by the other characters as inappropriate. Since Harriet's parentage is unknown, Emma believes that Harriet may have noble blood and encourages her to reject what turns out to be a more appropriate match with Robert Martin. By the time it is revealed that Harriet is the daughter of a tradesman, Emma admits that Mr. Martin is more suitable for her friend.

The relationship between marriage and social status creates hardship for other characters. Frank Churchill must keep his engagement to the orphan Jane Fairfax secret because his wealthy aunt would disapprove. Jane, in the absence of a good match, is forced to consider taking the position of a governess. The unmarried

Miss Bates is threatened with increasing poverty without a husband to take care of her and her mother. Finally, the match between Emma and Mr. Knightley is considered a good one not only because they are well matched in temperament but also because they are well matched in social class.

THE CONFINED NATURE OF WOMEN'S EXISTENCE

The novel's limited, almost claustrophobic scope of action gives us a strong sense of the confined nature of a woman's existence in early-nineteenth-century rural England. Emma possesses a great deal of intelligence and energy, but the best use she can make of these is to attempt to guide the marital destinies of her friends, a project that gets her into trouble. The alternative pastimes depicted in the book—social visits, charity visits, music, artistic endeavors—seem relatively trivial, at times even monotonous. Isabella is the only mother focused on in the story, and her portrayal suggests that a mother's life offers a woman little use of her intellect. Yet, when Jane compares the governess profession to the slave trade, she makes it clear that the life of a working woman is in no way preferable to the idleness of a woman of fortune. The novel focuses on marriage because marriage offers women a chance to exert their power, if only for a brief time, and to affect their own destinies without adopting the labors or efforts of the working class. Participating in the rituals of courtship and accepting or rejecting proposals is perhaps the most active role that women are permitted to play in Emma's world.

THE BLINDING POWER OF IMAGINATION

The novel offers sharply critical illustrations of the ways in which personal biases or desires blind objective judgment. Emma cannot understand the motives that guide Mr. Elton's behavior because she imagines that he is in love with Harriet. She later admits to herself that "[s]he had taken up the idea, she supposed, and made everything bend to it." Meanwhile, Mr. Elton's feelings for Emma cause him to mistake her behavior for encouragement. The generally infallible Mr. Knightley cannot form an unbiased judgment of Frank Churchill because he is jealous of Frank's claim on Emma, and Emma speaks cruelly of Jane because her vanity makes her jealous of Jane's accomplishments. Emma's biases cause her to invent an attachment between Harriet and Frank and blind her to the fact that Harriet actually has feelings for Knightley. At the same time, Frank's desire to use Emma as a screen for his real preference causes him to believe mistakenly that she is aware of the situation between him and Jane. The admirable, frequently ironic detachment of the narrator allows us to see many of these misunderstandings before the characters do, along with the humorous aspects of their behavior. And the plot is powered by a series of realizations that permit each character to make fuller, more objective judgments.

The Obstacles to Open Expression

The misunderstandings that permeate the novel are created, in part, by the conventions of social propriety. To differing degrees, characters are unable to express their feelings directly and openly, and their feelings are therefore mistaken. While the novel by no means suggests that the manners and rituals of social interaction should be eliminated, Austen implies that the overly clever, complex speech of Mr. Elton, Frank Churchill, and Emma deserves censure. She presents Mr. Martin's natural, warm, and direct manner of expressing himself as preferable to Mr. Elton's ostentatious and insincere style of complimenting people. Frank too possesses a talent for telling people exactly what they want to hear, and Knightley's suspicions of Frank's integrity are proven valid when it turns out that Frank has been misleading Highbury and hiding his true feelings for Jane. The cleverness of Frank's and Emma's banter gets them both into trouble by upsetting Jane, about whom Emma says indiscreet and unfair things. Emma and Frank's flirting at the Box Hill party hurts both Knightley and Jane. Moreover, Emma forgets herself to the extent that she cruelly insults Miss Bates. Austen seems to prefer Knightley and Martin's tactful tacitness to the sometimes overly gregarious commentary of Emma, Mr. Elton, and Frank, and, as a result, the author gives the latter characters' contrived speech a misleading influence on the story as a whole.

Motifs

Motifs are recurring structures, contrasts, or literary devices that can help to develop and inform the text's major themes.

Visits

The main events of the novel take place during visits that the characters pay to each other. The frequency and length of visits between characters indicates the level of intimacy and attachment between them. Frank's frequent visits to Hartfield show his relationship with

Emma to be close, though in hindsight we recognize that Frank also continually finds excuses to visit Jane. Mr. Knightley's constant presence at Hartfield indicates his affection and regard for Emma. Emma encourages Harriet to limit a visit with the Martin family to fifteen minutes, because such a short visit clearly indicates that any former interest has been lost. Emma is chastised for her failure to visit Miss Bates and Jane more often; when she takes steps to rectify this situation, she indicates a new concern for Miss Bates and a new regard for Jane.

PARTIES

More formal than visits, parties are organized around social conventions more than around individual attachments—Emma's hosting a dinner party for Mrs. Elton, a woman she dislikes, exemplifies this characteristic. There are six important parties in the novel: the Christmas Eve party at Randalls, the dinner party at the Coles', the dinner party given for Mrs. Elton, the dance at the Crown Inn, the morning party at Donwell Abbey, and the picnic at Box Hill. Each occasion provides the opportunity for social intrigue and misunderstandings, and for vanities to be satisfied and connections formed. Parties also give characters the chance to observe other people's interactions. Knightley observes Emma's behavior toward Frank and Frank's behavior toward Jane. Parties are microcosms of the social interactions that make up the novel as a whole.

CONVERSATIONAL SUBTEXTS

Much of the dialogue in *Emma* has double or even triple meanings, with different characters interpreting a single comment in different ways. Sometimes these double meanings are apparent to individual characters, and sometimes they are apparent only to the alert reader. For example, when Mr. Elton says of Emma's portrait of Harriet, "I cannot keep my eyes from it," he means to compliment Emma, but she thinks he is complimenting Harriet. When, during the scene in which Mr. Knightley proposes to Emma, Emma says, "I seem to have been doomed to blindness," Knightley believes she speaks of her blindness to Frank's love of Jane, but she actually refers to her blindness about her own feelings. One of our main tasks in reading the novel is to decode all of the subtexts underlying seemingly casual interactions, just as the main characters must. The novel concludes by unraveling the mystery behind who loves whom, which allows us to understand Austen's subtext more fully.

Symbols

Symbols are objects, characters, figures, or colors used to represent abstract ideas or concepts.

The Riddle
Also known as charades, riddles in the novel take the form of elaborate wordplay. They symbolize the pervasive subtexts that wait to be decoded in characters' larger social interactions. In Chapter 9, Mr. Elton presents a riddle to Emma and Harriet. Emma decodes it immediately, as "courtship," but she decodes it wrongly in the sense that she believes it is meant for Harriet rather than herself. This wordplay also makes an appearance during the Box Hill party, when Mr. Weston makes an acrostic for Emma.

The Word Game
Similar to the riddle, a word game is played in Chapter 41 between Emma, Frank, and Jane. It functions as a metaphor for the partial understandings and misunderstandings that exist among Emma, Frank, Jane, and Mr. Knightley. As Mr. Knightley looks on, Frank uses child's blocks to create words for the ladies to decode, though these words mean different things to each of them. Frank makes the word "blunder," which Jane understands as referring to a mistake he has just made, but whose meaning is opaque to Emma and Knightley. He then makes the word "Dixon," which Emma understands as a joke on Jane, and which baffles Knightley. In truth, everyone "blunders" in different ways that evening, because no one possesses complete enough information to interpret correctly everything that is going on.

Tokens of Affection
A number of objects in the novel take on symbolic significance as tokens of affection. Mr. Elton frames Emma's portrait of Harriet as a symbol of affection for her, though Emma misunderstands it as a symbol of affection for Harriet. Harriet keeps court plaster and a pencil stub as souvenirs of Mr. Elton. When the engagement between Jane and Frank is briefly called off, she returns his letters to symbolize her relinquishment of his affection.

SUMMARY & ANALYSIS

CHAPTERS 1–3

SUMMARY: CHAPTER 1

> *The real evils, indeed, of Emma's situation were the*
> *power of having rather too much her own way, and a*
> *disposition to think a little too well of herself....*
> *(See* QUOTATIONS, *p. 66)*

The narrator opens the novel by introducing us to Emma Wood-house, a girl endowed with "some of the best blessings of exist-ence," including good looks, intelligence, riches, and an affectionate father. Emma's only disadvantages are that she is slightly spoiled and that she thinks "a little too well of herself." Emma's mother died before Emma could form many memories of her, but her gentle governess, Miss Taylor, provided a motherly love. After Emma's older sister, Isabella, was married and moved to London, Miss Tay-lor and Emma became best friends.

As the novel begins, Miss Taylor has just left Hartfield, the estate of Emma and Mr. Woodhouse, to marry a widower named Mr. Weston, and Emma is left without a companion. She attempts to comfort her despondent father, who hates change, with the thought that they will see the new Mrs. Weston often, but Emma only par-tially succeeds in comforting herself. At this moment, neighborhood resident Mr. Knightley, the brother of Isabella's husband, pays a visit, having returned from visiting their mutual relations in Lon-don. He affirms the appropriateness of the match between Mr. Weston and Miss Taylor and gently chides Emma when she claims credit. Emma declares that she will repeat her matchmaking success by finding a wife for Mr. Elton, the village rector.

SUMMARY: CHAPTER 2

The narrator recounts Mr. Weston's history. His first marriage was to a woman named Miss Churchill, who came from a higher class than his. They had a son, named Frank, but the marriage was over-shadowed by the disapproval of Mrs. Weston's brother and sister-in-law, Mr. and Mrs. Churchill. When Mrs. Weston died after three years of marriage, Frank was essentially adopted by Mr. and Mrs.

Churchill and made their heir. Mr. Weston, left impoverished by the expectations of his first wife, spent the next twenty years of his life rebuilding his fortune. He eventually purchased Randalls, the small estate where he lives with the second Mrs. Weston.

The village has always been curious to see Frank Churchill, who writes a kind letter to Mrs. Weston indicating that he will pay a visit to his father and stepmother.

SUMMARY: CHAPTER 3

The Woodhouses give a small dinner party, to which they invite other members of their social circle: the widow Mrs. Bates; her single, middle-aged daughter, Miss Bates; and Mrs. Goddard, the mistress of the local boarding school. Mrs. Goddard brings one of her boarders, Harriet Smith, a girl whose parentage is unknown. Emma admires Harriet for her beauty and for her respect of Emma and Hartfield. She resolves to pursue friendship with Harriet, and to improve the naïve girl by detaching her from the inferior acquaintance of the farming Martin family. She plans to introduce Harriet to higher society.

ANALYSIS: CHAPTERS 1–3

The narration of these opening chapters creates a complicated portrait of Emma as a young, beautiful, clever, and confident character who exercises her influence in a constricted and complex environment and has much to learn about friendship, love, and the ways of the world. Emma's affection for Miss Taylor and her kindness to her foolish and somewhat tiresome father reveal Emma's capacity for true warmth and generosity. But, at the same time, the narrator quickly alerts us to the ways in which Emma is spoiled by her advantages and blinded by her own self-regard. Most explicitly, we are told at the novel's beginning:

> The real evils, indeed, of Emma's situation were the power of having rather too much her own way, and a disposition to think a little too well of herself: these were the disadvantages which threatened alloy to her many enjoyments. The danger, however, was at present so unperceived, that they did not by any means rank as misfortunes with her.

The novel's plot concerns Emma's education, as she gradually perceives the dangers that her own self-satisfaction presents.

The narrator also portrays Emma's weaknesses in more subtle ways, such as through irony. For example, the narrator hints that although Emma's friendship with Miss Taylor is clearly a pleasure to them both, a stricter and more authoritative governess might have been better for Emma's moral education. Emma's tendency to be self-serving in her choice of friends is shown contemptibly in her attraction to Harriet Smith. Emma likes Harriet for a purely superficial reason—her good looks—while recognizing that Harriet is not particularly intelligent. Most of all, she likes Harriet for being impressed with her, which she takes as evidence of Harriet's "good sense."

The question of Austen's loyalty to her protagonist is not easily resolved. Emma's independent fortune and unquestioned status within her village community are advantages that were unavailable to Austen herself, so it is easy to imagine Austen writing about Emma's self-important freedom with a certain amount of resentment. At the same time, however, the novel takes place mostly from Emma's point of view—if we disliked Emma, the novel would be unreadable. The narrative structure of the novel complicates things further—the narrator is omniscient, qualified to pass judgment on Emma with commentary that is often tinged with irony, but the narrator also frequently takes up Emma's point of view, sometimes almost merging the two.

When the narrator explains Emma's commitment to Harriet's betterment, commenting that the project "would be an interesting, and certainly a very kind undertaking; highly becoming [Emma's] own situation in life, her leisure, and powers," she uses a narrative technique called free indirect discourse, for which Austen is well known. When using free indirect discourse, the narrator steps into and out of characters' thoughts, using language that sounds just like what the character would say, except that the narrator does not place it in quotation marks. The narrator's use of free indirect discourse creates irony, as it becomes difficult to tell when the seemingly approving narrator is actually pointing to flaws in her characters. For instance, in the preceding quote, the narrator seems to express approval of Emma's decision to take on Harriet as a project. Yet, because the words are expressed in Emma's language, not the narrator's, it seems that we are meant to view the statement with skepticism and to note that Emma's seeming selflessness stems from the desire to make herself look good, to fill her spare time, and to exercise power.

The confined, limited nature of Emma's existence makes her a sympathetic character. There are few other residents who would be suitable company for the Woodhouses, the dominant family in the village. With Miss Taylor's departure, Emma is left with the prospect of spending most evenings without a companion other than her father. When she puts a party together, it is small, limited to Knightley, Mr. Elton, the Westons, the Bateses (noted for their dullness and predictability), and Mrs. Goddard. The excitement produced by the prospect of Frank Churchill's visit and Emma's immediate attachment to Harriet show how desperate she is for new acquaintances and experiences. The book focuses not only on Emma as an individual character but as a more general phenomenon: a young, intelligent, and active woman seeking to exercise her talents and abilities within her narrow scope of opportunity.

CHAPTERS 4–6

SUMMARY: CHAPTER 4
Emma and Harriet strike up an immediate intimacy as Harriet replaces Mrs. Weston as Emma's companion on her habitual walks. Emma remains unimpressed with Harriet's intelligence but appreciates her willingness to be guided. Emma encourages Harriet to tell everything about herself, and their conversation soon centers on the Martin family, which Harriet has visited frequently over the past two months. Emma is alarmed to learn that the family includes an eligible bachelor, Mr. Robert Martin, and fears that her friend may have feelings for him. A match between Harriet and Mr. Martin would be unacceptable to Emma because the Martins are farmers, and therefore, in her opinion, socially beneath her new friend. She discourages Harriet from thinking well of Mr. Martin by asking questions about his education and predicting that any wife Mr. Martin takes will be too inferior to merit friendship with Harriet. After they run into Mr. Martin on one of their walks, Emma encourages Harriet to compare his manners with those of the gentlemen they know, praising Mr. Elton's manners as particularly genteel. The narrator reveals that Emma determined during the party at Hartfield to encourage a match between Harriet and Mr. Elton.

SUMMARY: CHAPTER 5
Mr. Knightley and Mrs. Weston converse about Emma's new friendship with Harriet. Knightley believes that the friendship is danger-

ous for both parties. Harriet's flattery, Knightley suspects, will reinforce Emma's self-regard, while Emma's influence will injure Harriet's happiness, because Harriet "will grow just refined enough to be uncomfortable with those among whom birth and circumstance have placed her home." Mrs. Weston disagrees, believing that Emma needs Harriet's companionship and that Emma's company will improve Harriet. She advises Knightley to keep his mouth shut, and the conversation ends with speculation about what will become of Emma. Noting Emma's declaration that she will never marry and her lack of suitable prospects, Knightley comments that he "should like to see Emma in love, and in some doubt of a return; it would do her good."

SUMMARY: CHAPTER 6
Emma continues to point out Mr. Elton's finer qualities to Harriet and is convinced that he is already in love with her friend. Mr. Elton praises the graces that Harriet has gained in Emma's company, and he quickly seconds Emma's idea to paint a watercolor portrait of Harriet. As Emma paints, Mr. Elton is only too attentive to her progress, and though Mrs. Weston and Mr. Knightley point out that Emma has exaggerated Harriet's beauty, Mr. Elton emphatically praises the portrait's likeness. He volunteers to take the watercolor to London to be framed. All the while, Emma continues to believe that Mr. Elton's enthusiasm is for Harriet, though Mr. Elton makes comments on Emma's skill in rendering and improving on the beautiful subject.

ANALYSIS: CHAPTERS 4–6
Over the course of these three chapters, we learn that Emma is extremely class-conscious and also somewhat manipulative. She unattractively dismisses Robert Martin because of his social class, saying, "The yeomanry [the class of farmers who hold land under long- term leases] are precisely the order of people with whom I feel I can have nothing to do. A degree or two lower, and a creditable appearance might interest me; I might hope to be useful to their families in some way or another." In other words, Emma is only interested in people who are of her social class or so far beneath her that she might, from a comfortable position of superiority, flatter herself by being "useful" to them. Such superior usefulness is what Emma attempts with Harriet, and she even lies to her friend in order to manipulate her. Although Emma observes to herself that Mr. Mar-

tin's "appearance was very neat and he looked like a sensible young man," she tells Harriet, "He is very plain … remarkably plain, but that is nothing compared to his entire want of gentility."

Mr. Knightley and Mrs. Weston make Emma seem more likable than she makes herself seem. Because Knightley shows himself to have good sense, and also because he is the one character willing to find fault with Emma, he is the novel's most reliable mouthpiece for Austen's views of Emma. His discussion of Emma shows that he genuinely cares for her but views her as a child lacking sense and understanding rather than as an equal. He believes that Emma has been "spoiled by being the cleverest of her family" but respects her stubbornness and independence. He also admits that though Emma is very pretty, she is not vain about her looks; "her vanity lies another way." Knightley's pointed criticisms are offset by Mrs. Weston's dismissive remarks that Emma is a caring daughter, sister, and friend who "will make no lasting blunder."

Like Austen's narration, the dialogue between characters frequently contains a subtext available only to certain characters or to the reader. For instance, when Emma says to Harriet, "I wish you may not get into a scrape, Harriet, when ever [Mr. Martin] does marry—I mean as to being acquainted with his wife … it does not follow that he might marry anybody at all fit for you to notice," we admire the cleverness of Emma's suggestion to Harriet that Mr. Martin is beneath her, even as we disapprove of Emma's action. Chapter 6 is particularly rich in dialogue with subtext, as Mr. Elton's admiration for Emma is perceptible to us but not to Emma. For instance, when Mr. Elton tells Emma, "You have given Miss Smith all that she required…. She was a beautiful creature when she came to you; but, in my opinion, the attractions you have added are infinitely superior to what she received from nature," we hear Mr. Elton's emphasis on Emma's skills, but Emma can only hear his praise of Harriet.

CHAPTERS 7–9

SUMMARY: CHAPTER 7

Harriet receives a letter from Mr. Martin proposing marriage and goes directly to Emma to seek advice. Emma acts as if there is obviously no doubt that Harriet should not accept, and she proceeds to offer Harriet advice about the wording of her refusal. When it becomes clear that Harriet is doubtful about her answer, Emma becomes somewhat cold and disingenuously states, "I shall not give you any advice, Harriet. . . . This is a point which you must settle with your own feelings." When, under Emma's subtle guidance, Harriet states that she will probably reject Mr. Martin, Emma immediately congratulates her friend on having made the right decision and points out that if Harriet had accepted him, then Emma would no longer be able to be her friend. Harriet immediately affirms that the loss of Emma is unthinkable, and the two of them draft a letter refusing the proposal. It is clear that Harriet is pained by her decision and cares for Mr. Martin, but Emma cheers her up with reminders of Mr. Elton.

SUMMARY: CHAPTER 8

With Harriet at Mrs. Goddard's preparing for an extended visit to Hartfield, Mr. Knightley and Emma have the opportunity for a lengthy conversation about Harriet and Mr. Martin. Knightley reveals that Mr. Martin has consulted him about proposing to Harriet, and Mr. Knightley makes it clear that he supports the match. Emma informs him that the proposal has already been made and rejected, and she insists that Mr. Martin is not Harriet's equal. Knightley very nearly loses his temper, and he insists upon Mr. Martin's superiority to Harriet in sense and "true gentility." Knightley is especially displeased by what he immediately guesses was Emma's role in the rejection, and he states flatly, "You have been no friend to Harriet Smith." Emma counters that Harriet's beauty and good temper, along with the possibility that she is the daughter of a gentleman, make her a desirable match. Knightley tells Emma that if she thinks Mr. Elton will marry Harriet, she is wrong, because Elton will only marry a woman with money. Vexed with one another, Emma and Knightley part ways. Emma is comforted by the return of Harriet, who has heard a rumor that Elton is on an important errand regarding a lady.

SUMMARY: CHAPTER 9

Emma and Harriet have been collecting riddles (also called "charades") into a scrapbook, and when Mr. Elton returns from London with the framed portrait of Harriet, he contributes one. Emma immediately decodes the riddle and sees that its answer is the word "courtship." She translates the riddle for Harriet, who could not solve it herself, but Harriet is nonetheless flattered by its meaning. Emma convinces Harriet that the riddle foretells a proposal, and she copies the riddle into Harriet's book. After some discussion among the family anticipating the upcoming Christmas visit of Isabella, Mr. John Knightley, and their children, Emma tells Mr. Elton that she has solved his charade and copied it into Harriet's book. Elton is clearly moved, and Emma concludes that his emotion comes from seeing his riddle in Harriet's book.

ANALYSIS: CHAPTERS 7–9

Chapters 7 and 8 adhere to a pattern already established by Chapters 4 and 5: first, we read a chapter that relates Emma's manipulation of Harriet; then we read a chapter offering Knightley's negative judgment of her actions. Chapter 7 again reveals Emma's gift for double-edged speech. While Harriet believes Emma's protestations of not wanting to influence Harriet's behavior, it is perfectly clear to us that everything Emma says is calculated to make Harriet reject Mr. Martin's proposal. However, Emma also has endearing moments of uncalculated honesty—when she admits to Harriet that Mr. Martin has written a better letter than she had expected, for example, even though this admission does not support Emma's plan to match Harriet with Mr. Elton.

Emma's conversation with Mr. Knightley, in Chapter 8, about Harriet and Mr. Martin, Austen may offer an implied criticism of what men look for in a wife. While Knightley suggests that good sense is the quality that men most value, Emma points out that most men would be content to have a wife as beautiful and good tempered as Harriet. When Emma comments, "I am very much mistaken if your sex in general would not think such beauty, and such temper, the highest claims a woman could possess," we may hear a slight bitterness in her words. Though the novel rewards good sense as the most important human virtue, Austen is aware that the marriage market often rewards more superficial qualities.

Sharing riddles was a common genteel pastime in the early nineteenth century, and the riddle in Chapter 9 serves as an important metaphor for the social interactions that define the novel as a whole. Emma is able to decode Mr. Elton's riddle immediately, while Harriet is comically helpless. Emma's manipulations of Harriet succeed because Harriet is unaware of the conscious, calculated nature of Emma's influence, even though it is perfectly discernible to us. In general, the novel contains two groups of characters: those who can read between the lines and those who cannot. As readers of the novel, we join the former group, and our ability to interpret hidden meaning guides our loyalties as we read. However, while the novel delights in wordplay on a stylistic level, on the level of ideas it prefers plain and honest feeling to overwrought expression. Austen juxtaposes Mr. Elton's ornate riddle and the plainness of Mr. Martin's letter, and while Emma and Harriet believe that Mr. Elton's riddle is much superior, Emma from time to time finds Elton's speech absurd in its rhetorical flourishes, as the closing sentences of Chapter 9 indicate.

The novel also showcases the danger posed by ornate speech—it is likely to be misunderstood. Though Emma is constantly searching for subtext because of her own calculating nature, she is not as good as she believes at reading between the social lines. She continually misreads Mr. Elton's behavior, to such an extent that we are tempted to question all of the insistence on Emma's "cleverness." Though Emma is often correct that there is more to situations than meets the eye, Harriet's simplicity sometimes makes her see obvious truths that the too-clever Emma misses. For instance, Harriet rightly perceives that Emma is more Mr. Elton's type than is she is, commenting, "You and Mr. Elton are one as clever as the other."

CHAPTERS 10–12

SUMMARY: CHAPTER 10
Emma and Harriet make a charitable visit to a poor family near Mr. Elton's vicarage. On the way, Harriet expresses her surprise that Emma has not married, and Emma explains her resolution to remain single. The poor family they assist engages their compassion, but soon the girls' thoughts turn to Mr. Elton, who meets them on the road. Emma attempts to leave Mr. Elton and Harriet together by falling behind, speaking with a child, and pretending to lace her boots. Using the need for new ribbon to lace her boots as an excuse, Emma requests that they stop at Mr. Elton's house at the vicarage, but even though Emma contrives to leave the would-be lovers alone there together, Elton fails to show interest in Harriet. Emma considers him slow but is not dissuaded in her plans.

SUMMARY: CHAPTER 11
Mr. and Mrs. John Knightley and their children arrive at Hartfield and temporarily occupy all of Emma's attention. Mr. Woodhouse and Isabella commiserate over losing Mrs. Weston, and there is speculation about whether Mr. Weston's son, Frank Churchill, will make his visit. Isabella is like her father in both tenderness and ner-

vousness, and Emma believes that Isabella's sharp-minded husband sometimes speaks too sternly to Isabella and to the family.

SUMMARY: CHAPTER 12

Mr. Knightley comes to dinner at Hartfield, and though he and Emma still disagree about Harriet, they reconcile. Knightley tells Emma that Mr. Martin has been terribly disappointed by Harriet's rejection. Isabella is filled in on all of the latest news from Highbury. She inquires after Jane Fairfax, Miss Bates's niece, and suggests that Jane would make a good companion for Emma.

The conversation turns to Mr. and Mrs. John Knightley's decision to go to Southend, a beach resort, instead of visiting the Woodhouses in the autumn. Mr. Woodhouse advocates the advice of a friend, Mr. Perry, who is an apothecary. All the while, Isabella maintains that her doctor, Mr. Wingfield, is more trustworthy. Emma tries to change the subject, and eventually Mr. John Knightley snaps that Perry should mind his own business. Emma and Mr. Knightley smooth things over.

ANALYSIS: CHAPTERS 10–12

When Emma visits the poor in Chapter 10, we see her desire to be "useful," which she has emphasized throughout the novel, fulfilled in a new way. Her aspiration to be active and do good in the world is noble, especially considering the fact that her riches and her beauty might have left her content to fill her days in frivolous pursuits. Yet, Emma's charitable acts—for example, the guidance she offers Harriet—often stem from her own vanity and are therefore harmful as well as helpful. The narrator clearly contrasts Emma's romantic, misguided attitude toward Harriet with her attitude toward the poor, writing,

> She understood their ways, could allow for their ignorance and their temptations, had no romantic expectations of extraordinary virtue from those for whom education had done so little, entered into their troubles with ready sympathy, and always gave her assistance with as much intelligence as good-will.

Austen seems to signal that in this sphere, a woman with Emma's privilege and advantages can actually do good. The fact that Emma displays the capacity for genuine empathy and for a usefulness that exercises her intelligence more than her vanity bodes well for her improvement.

As Emma and Harriet depart, Emma undermines her goodwill by describing the poor as picturesque—"These are sights, Harriet, to do one good. . . . I feel now as if I could think of nothing but these poor creatures all the rest of the day." However, Emma exhibits that she is aware of her fickleness and vanity when she adds, "[A]nd yet who can say how soon it may all vanish from my mind?" Emma's mixture of self-delusion and self-knowledge is complex, and it is ambiguous how much credit we are meant to give her for her assistance to the poor and how much condemnation she deserves for her rapid return to obliviousness.

In chapters 11 and 12, Austen provides context for Emma's repudiation of marriage by focusing on the marriage with which Emma is most familiar—that of her sister and Mr. John Knightley. Isabella's attentiveness to her children, husband, and father are admirable, but the novel's treatment of Isabella as a simpler, less dynamic woman than her sister implies that it does not take very much intelligence or vigor to be a good wife and mother. Furthermore, Isabella and John's gender-typical behavior is somewhat boring, as the two seem to lack the sort of charisma and personality we see in Emma and Mr. Knightley. Isabella is caring, emotional, and somewhat silly and weak, while John is rational and purposeful but too willing to damage the feelings of others.

As they conspire to keep the family peace, Emma and Mr. Knightley compare favorably to their siblings. Though Mr. Knightley is more reasonable and dignified than high-spirited, impulsive Emma, they share a similar intelligence and get along with each other very well. Their relationship does not seem to be built upon gender stereotypes, and their amiability suggests that Emma might in fact be satisfied in a married life.

CHAPTERS 13–15

SUMMARY: CHAPTER 13

The Woodhouses and Knightleys are invited to the Westons' for Christmas Eve dinner. Harriet and Mr. Elton are also included, but Harriet comes down with a sore throat and is forced to miss the gathering. Emma meets Mr. Elton while visiting Harriet and is pleased by his attentions to her friend, but she remains puzzled that he refuses her suggestion to skip the party since Harriet will not be there. Mr. John Knightley witnesses the exchange and suggests to Emma that Mr. Elton has feelings for her. Amused, Emma dismisses the suggestion. When she and Mr. Elton travel to the gathering in the same carriage, she is surprised that Mr. Elton's concern for Harriet gives way to cheerful anticipation of the evening ahead.

SUMMARY: CHAPTER 14
Entering the party, Emma attempts to put Mr. Elton's strange behavior out of her mind, but his constant hovering presence makes her worry that Mr. John Knightley's suggestion that Mr. Elton cares for her may be correct. Meanwhile, Mr. Weston announces that Frank Churchill is due to visit in early January. Emma feels some interest in this news because she has half-seriously thought of Frank as a potential suitor, though she does not anticipate giving up her vow to remain single. Mrs. Weston confides to Emma that she has some anxiety about meeting her stepson, and she fears Mrs. Churchill will prevent him from coming. She and Emma speculate about the situation at Enscombe, the Churchill estate, and Emma wonders why a young man should be so dependent upon the impulses of his guardian.

SUMMARY: CHAPTER 15
Mr. Elton joins Emma in the drawing room and displeases her by acting more concerned with her health than with Harriet's. John Knightley's report that it has begun snowing leads to a small crisis, and Mr. Woodhouse and Isabella are beside themselves with worry about traveling the three-quarters of a mile home. Mr. Knightley assesses the situation and reassures everyone that they will make it back safely.

In the confusion created by the party breaking up, Emma finds herself alone in one of the carriages with Mr. Elton. He immediately declares his love for her and proposes. Hoping that he is merely drunk, Emma attempts to remind him that Harriet is the true object of his affections. Astonished, Elton assures Emma that he has never been interested in Harriet. Moreover, he is convinced that Emma has known of and encouraged his sentiments. Emma sharply rebukes him and refuses his proposal, and the two travel the remainder of the journey in angry silence.

ANALYSIS: CHAPTERS 13–15
Emma's belief that she is different from others cannot merely be attributed to her sense of superiority; it also results from her ambi-

tion to make her life more interesting and more useful than the limitations of village life seem to allow. Observing and imagining the destinies of other lives exercises her intellect. We might think of Emma as a kind of novelist creating plots for the characters that people her world. In this sense, she may be closer to Austen than her mistakes would lead us to believe. In fact, Emma is somewhat prudish, afraid to consider marriage for herself, despite her belief that "a good match" is the key to happiness for her friends. Alert to what she believes are the subtleties of flirtation between Harriet and Mr. Elton, she is incapable or unwilling to see that she might be engaging in such social games herself.

Emma's confrontation with Mr. Elton is the novel's first major crisis. The true turning point is not Elton's proposal, however, but his accusation that Emma has known that she was the object of his affections all along. He says, "I am sure you have seen and understood me," and for the first time in the novel Emma is at a loss for words, fiercely angry. This is the first instance in which Emma is implicated in the social interactions that she believed she was manipulating from a position of control and detachment. She has understood her own calculating behavior as beyond reproach, in a sense invisible, and suddenly she is seen and placed within the society from which she believed she has separated herself, forced to realize that she has been lying to both Harriet and herself.

Austen has sometimes been accused of a failure of nerve when it comes to depicting emotional scenes because she generally switches from dialogue to indirect language when relating moments of passion. Instead of reporting Elton's speech directly, Austen writes, "Mr. Elton [had] actually [begun] making violent love to her: availing himself of the precious opportunity, declaring sentiments which must be already well known, hoping-fearing-adoring-ready to die if she refused him. . . ." From this statement and from what we know of Mr. Elton, we can imagine his actual words, but their shock value is softened by the indirect description. The information Austen gives us about Emma's feelings is similarly vague: "It would be impossible to say what Emma felt on hearing this; which of all her unpleasant sensations was uppermost." It is up to us to decide whether such language weakens the effect of these scenes or makes them more powerful by preserving the characters' privacy and challenging us to supply the emotional details.

CHAPTERS 16–18

SUMMARY: CHAPTER 16

*The first error . . . was foolish, it was wrong, to take so
active a part in bringing any two people together.*
(See QUOTATIONS, p. 66)

Back at Hartfield after her ride with Mr. Elton, Emma plunges into
self-recrimination as she looks back over the past weeks. Her big-
gest regret concerns Harriet, whose feelings for Elton, Emma realizes, are due mostly to Emma's own encouragement. She decides she
need not pity Elton, because the artificiality of his addresses suggests
that he was more interested in her fortune than in herself. She realizes that both of the Knightley brothers have been right about Elton
and that she has been wrong all along. Emma vows to give up
matchmaking, but she cannot stop herself from searching for a new
suitor for Harriet.

The next morning, Emma is comforted by the reflection that nei-
ther Elton's nor Harriet's feelings could have been very strong and
by the fact that no one else needs to know what has happened. Several days of snow provide a respite, as everyone stays at home, but
Emma dreads telling Harriet what has happened.

SUMMARY: CHAPTER 17

Mr. and Mrs. John Knightley return to London, and Mr. Elton
writes Mr. Woodhouse to announce that he will spend the next few
weeks in the town of Bath. Relieved, Emma immediately visits Harriet to explain what has happened. Emma's sense of her own failures, and Harriet's modesty and sweetness in taking the news, give
Emma the temporary impression that Harriet, rather than herself, is
"the superior creature." She moves Harriet to Hartfield and
attempts to comfort her and drive Elton out of Harriet's mind.
Emma tries to prepare Harriet for the inevitable moment when they
will see Elton in their social circle after he returns from Bath.

SUMMARY: CHAPTER 18

Frank Churchill does not make his expected visit, to the disappointment of Mrs. Weston in particular. Emma, preoccupied with her
other worries, does not mind, but she feels she must express disappointment so that she will appear her usual self. Her warmth in
doing so gets her into an argument with Mr. Knightley about the
young man. Knightley expresses the same thought Emma has

expressed: how can a twenty-four-year-old man be prevented by his aunt from doing his duty? In reply, Emma suggests that Knightley is a poor judge of "the difficulties of dependence." She expresses her sympathies for Frank's situation and her conviction that he would come if he could, but Knightley counters that no sensible, honorable man would be prevented from doing his duty. Emma predicts that Frank, when he does arrive in Highbury, will be perfectly charming. Knightley believes that Frank will be superficial and insufferable, and Knightley's prejudice against the stranger surprises Emma.

ANALYSIS: CHAPTERS 16–18

Chapter 16 is remarkable because, unlike most of the novel's other chapters, it deals almost exclusively with Emma's thoughts and feelings, her inner life. On the whole, Emma seems to have gained a measure of understanding, but the narrator has provided hints that she has more to learn. We see her grow in humility and selflessness as, shaken by Elton's proposal, she thinks that she would have gladly undergone an even greater blow to her ego, if only she could have avoided hurting Harriet. In addition to increased self-understanding, Emma shows an increased understanding of Elton's character as "proud, assuming, conceited; very full of his own claims, and little concerned about the feelings of others."

However, Emma has not totally shed her former shortcomings. Emma's resolution to cease matchmaking is put in terms that suggest she has gained a good deal of insight: "It was foolish, it was wrong, to take so active a part in bringing two people together. It was adventuring too far, assuming too much, making light of what ought to be serious—a trick of what ought to be simple." But soon she is imagining new matches for Harriet, though she stops herself with the recognition of her own relapse. Emma's reflection that "there had been no real affection either in [Elton's] language or manners" shows her continued sense of the superiority of her mind and manners to Elton's. She blames Elton probably more than he deserves for her own mistakes, and her quick assumption that his feelings for her were insincere seems self-serving. Her revised understanding of Elton is accurate, but her refusal to implicate herself as party to his misunderstanding shows that Emma's self-understanding is not complete.

Although the argument Emma and Mr. Knightley have about Frank Churchill seems silly, since Emma argues feelingly for a position she does not really hold and because Knightley makes harsh judgments about a man he has never met, Knightley's comments provide real insight into his feelings. Because the usually calm and prudent Knightley is so unnecessarily vexed by a stranger, we begin to suspect that something more is bothering Knightley. Emma thinks Knightley's anger is "unworthy of the real liberality of mind" that we expect from him. In hindsight, it is clear that his vexation stems from subconscious jealousy and marks the beginnings of his romantic feelings for Emma, but in the meantime we remain as mystified as she.

In describing Emma's quarrel with Knightley, the narrator indirectly comments on society's treatment of different genders by contrasting Emma's and Knightley's views, which underscore the different opportunities that society makes available to women and men. The narrator contrasts Emma's insistence on the "difficulties of dependence" and the subtle, complex, and powerful influence that family obligations can have upon one's freedom, with Knightley's insistence that men who think rightly should act resolutely and will not encounter real opposition if they do so. Clearly, Emma's vision and understanding of family dependence is a product of her observations and experiences as a woman, and it seems that she may be arguing more about herself than about Frank. Knightley's vision of and insistence upon resolute action, on the other hand, is a strictly masculine view of correct and plausible behavior.

CHAPTERS 19–21

SUMMARY: CHAPTER 19
During a walk, Emma has little success turning Harriet's thoughts from Mr. Elton and therefore decides that they should call on Mrs. and Miss Bates, a duty that Emma usually shuns. During their visit, they are forced to hear about Mr. Elton and his travels, and though Emma has tried to time her visit so as to avoid hearing about Miss Bates's niece, Jane Fairfax, Miss Bates produces a letter from Jane, who lives with her guardians, Colonel and Mrs. Campbell. The Campbells are about to visit their newly married daughter, Mrs. Dixon, in Ireland, which means that Jane will be coming for an extended visit in Highbury in a week's time. Based on slight evidence, Emma suspects that there has been a romance between Jane and the Campbells' daughter's husband, Mr. Dixon, and that this is the reason that Jane is missing the trip to Ireland.

SUMMARY & ANALYSIS

SUMMARY: CHAPTER 20

Jane's history is given, starting from how, at age three, she became an orphan after her father was killed in battle and her mother died of consumption and grief. Jane lived with her aunt and grandmother in Highbury until she was eight years old. Then, a friend of her father's, Colonel Campbell, took an interest in her well-being and made her part of his household. He provided her with an education, but, since he would be unable to give her an inheritance, it was understood that when Jane came of age she would become a governess. Meanwhile, Jane became dear to the Campbell family and enjoyed the pleasures of elegant society in London. Her stay in Highbury constitutes her last taste of freedom before becoming a governess.

Jane arrives, and Emma greets the girl's return after two years' absence with mixed feelings. She has never liked Jane, for reasons she cannot fully explain (Mr. Knightley suggests to her that she is jealous), but Jane's beauty impresses her, and she feels compassion for her impending fate. Soon the dullness of Jane's companions, along with Jane's reserve, confirms Emma's dislike. Emma discovers that Jane has known Frank Churchill in Weymouth, but Jane divulges little information about him.

SUMMARY: CHAPTER 21

Just as Mr. Knightley is about to give Emma some news, the Bateses arrive with Jane to thank the Woodhouses for the hindquarter of pork they have sent; they manage to precede Knightley in divulging that Mr. Elton is to marry a Miss Hawkins. Emma is caught off guard, and Mr. Knightley's looks suggest he knows something of what has transpired between them. However, she soon regains enough composure to make another failed attempt to engage Jane in conversation. The company departs, and Harriet bursts in with news that she has run into Mr. Martin and his sister in town. She relates that after some awkwardness, the pair greeted her with kindness, leaving Harriet flustered. Emma is impressed by the Martins' behavior and briefly second-guesses her judgment of them, but she concludes that their station in life is still too low for Harriet. She is only able to distract Harriet from the episode by sharing the news of Mr. Elton's impending marriage.

ANALYSIS: CHAPTERS 19–21

Miss Bates's repetitious speeches, and the mileage she can get from a single letter or piece of news from someone outside of Highbury, strongly reinforce our sense of the claustrophobia of village life. Though the character of Miss Bates is considered a comic master-piece, there is also a pathetic and even alarming quality to the nar-rowness of her experience. In contrast to more sophisticated and calculating characters such as Emma and Mr. Knightley, who con-ceal or reveal what they are thinking depending upon the appropri-ateness of the situation and the effect they wish to produce, Miss Bates narrates everything that passes through her head, all of it more or less harmless.

With a more developed sense of Miss Bates's character, Austen provides some distinctly different views of women's experience in Highbury. She makes an implicit statement about intelligence and its potential for creating hardship when she contrasts Emma and Miss Bates. For instance, Miss Bates speaks in absurdly long, digres-sive sentences, interrupting herself frequently and often forgetting her point. In one example, she says:

> I was reading [Jane's letter] to Mrs. Cole, and, since she went away, I was reading it again to my mother, for it is such a pleasure to her—a letter from Jane—that she can never hear it often enough; so I knew it could not be far off, and here it is, only just under my housewife—and since you are so kind as to wish to hear what she says—but, first of all, I really must, in justice to Jane, apologise for her writing so short a letter—only two pages, you see hardly two, and in general she fills the whole paper and crosses half.

Forced to read these complex and boring details, we share Emma's impatience with Miss Bates but suspect, with Mr. Knightley, that Emma should greet Miss Bates with greater charity and less irrita-tion. Margaret Drabble, in an introductory essay on the novel, sug-gests that Miss Bates might be read as a stand-in for Austen herself. Single, middle-aged, dependent, caring for an elderly mother, Miss Bates's situation in life is much closer to Austen's at the time she was writing the novel than is Emma's. Of course, Austen is much more intelligent than the character she creates, so perhaps Miss Bates exemplifies Austen's imagination of what her life would be like without her intellect. The picture is somewhat alarming, because Miss Bates's ignorance means that she is perfectly contented with the life she leads. Perhaps Austen means for us to understand that intelligence, at least for a woman in the early nineteenth century, can be as much a source of suffering as of solace.

Once she has sworn off her aggressive matchmaking, Emma compensates by reconstructing what she thinks must be the interesting and provocative circumstances that brought Jane to Highbury. While Emma has learned, at least for the time being, not to orchestrate the love lives of those around her, the restlessness of her mind ignites her imagination and endangers her ability to observe others accurately. She bases her suspicion that Jane and Mr. Dixon had an attachment before his marriage to Mrs. Campbell on the slightest circumstantial evidence, and this mistaken impression of Jane will have greater negative consequences. Though Austen must understand imagination to be a gift, in particular the gift that makes it possible for her to write, here she suggests that a careless exercise of the imagination can be dangerous.

CHAPTERS 22–24

SUMMARY: CHAPTER 22

In Highbury, there is great speculation about Miss Hawkins, Mr. Elton's fiancée. Mr. Elton returns to the village long enough to confirm the rumors that his bride-to-be is beautiful, accomplished, and of some fortune. Emma is relieved that his marriage will ease the awkwardness of his return to their social circle, but she has some uncharitable thoughts about Miss Hawkins's inferior connections. She has difficulty persuading Harriet to share her coolness, however. Only the topic of Mr. Martin puts Mr. Elton out of Harriet's mind.

Harriet is flustered when Mr. Martin's sister leaves her a note at Mrs. Goddard's. Emma decides that Harriet should return the visit but stay only a brief time in order to reinforce the distance that Emma, despite a twinge of conscience, believes Harriet must maintain from the Martin family.

SUMMARY: CHAPTER 23

Emma takes Harriet to visit the Martins. Ahead of time, they agree that Emma is to return and retrieve Harriet after fifteen minutes. Harriet has a friendly and emotional visit with Mr. Martin's mother and sister, but when the visit is cut short, it is clear the Martins understand that they have been slighted. Though pained, Emma still believes she is doing what is best for Harriet.

Emma's spirits are revived by a meeting with Mr. and Mrs. Weston, who bring the news that Frank Churchill's arrival is imminent. The following day, Emma unexpectedly meets Frank at Hartfield, and she is pleased to find that he is very good-looking, bright, and charming. Frank has just the right compliment for everyone, especially Mrs. Weston, which pleases Emma. Emma can see that Mr. Weston hopes that she and Frank might form an attachment, and she wonders if the thought has occurred to Frank. When his father departs on an errand, Frank leaves to call on his acquaintance from Weymouth, Jane Fairfax.

SUMMARY: CHAPTER 24

Frank Churchill and Mrs. Weston visit Hartfield the next day, and Emma is pleased by Frank's warmth toward his stepmother. He seems genuinely interested in everything about Highbury as the three walk about the village, especially in the sites that are meaningful to his father. Encountering an unused ballroom, he suggests that they should organize a dance, and he dismisses Emma's protestations about the village's lack of worthy families.

Emma inquires about Frank's visit with the Bateses, and the two share impressions of Jane. Frank says that he finds her unattractive and reserved. He thinks, however, that she is a talented musician and affirms that they saw a good deal of each other in Weymouth. Emma shares her theory about Jane and Mr. Dixon, which Frank seems to resist, but then he gives in to Emma's greater knowledge of Jane. On the whole, Emma finds Frank even more to her liking than she expected, possessing his father's warmth and sociability and lacking the proud airs one might acquire from the Churchills.

ANALYSIS: CHAPTERS 22–24

Though our position with respect to Emma is privileged—the narrator often provides details that allow us to know more about Emma than she knows about herself—the subjectivity of other characters is barely highlighted at all, making it difficult for us to understand their true dispositions and motives any more than Emma does. With hindsight (the novel must be reread to fully appreciate Austen's subtleties), all of Frank Churchill's comments and actions become transparent, but without it, we, like Emma, have to be taught how to reach the correct interpretations. From this point in the novel forward, we can no longer witness Emma's education with detachment; Austen structures her book so that we must share it.

As Emma had predicted in her argument with Mr. Knightley, Frank has a talent for guessing which line of conversation and compliment will please each person, and Frank tailors his behavior accordingly. Remembering Mr. Knightley's initial distaste for Frank's demeanor, we wonder if Frank's talent at compliments is altogether as admirable as it seems. Though Emma may be skeptical of Frank's remarks, she gives him the benefit of the doubt because she believes he has a kind nature and is impressed by his speech. She recognizes that Frank's compliments to Mr. and Mrs. Weston are exaggerated, but Emma believes they express genuine gratitude and affection and forgives his exaggeration because it stems from his honorable desire to please. When Frank claims that he has always longed to come to Highbury, Emma wonders why he has not come sooner, but she dismisses her skepticism by concluding, "[I]f it were a falsehood, it was a pleasant one, and pleasantly handled."

Emma exhibits a healthy detachment during her first meeting with Frank. Where another young woman might manifest admiration for Frank, knowing that others think he may be a proper suitor for her, she expresses reserve: "She must see more of him to understand his ways; at present she only felt they were agreeable." Whether Emma has affectionate interest for Frank at this point is irrelevant—it would be inappropriate for a reputable woman of her position to display too much interest in a man this early.

Frank's inconsistent attitude toward Jane Fairfax is the most confusing part of his behavior. An alert reader will suspect that something unusual has passed between Frank and Jane, but it is only on a second reading that we recognize Frank's behavior as a complicated mixture of honesty and outright deception, vulnerability and manipulation. At this point, he is a good enough liar to fool Emma. At first Frank seems in a rush to visit Jane, but then he is surprisingly willing to postpone the visit. He is unexpectedly firm in refusing the assistance of Mr. Woodhouse's servant in finding her house, and his insistence on Jane's unattractiveness is uncharacteristically rude. He attempts to avoid Emma's question about his relationship to Jane by ducking into a store, but then he himself returns to the subject. The first time we see Frank at a loss for words is when Emma shares her suspicion that Jane has had a relationship with Mr. Dixon. However, Frank recovers his composure enough to assess how well Emma actually knows Jane by asking her more questions.

CHAPTERS 25–27

SUMMARY: CHAPTER 25

Emma's good opinion of Frank Churchill is injured when he makes a day trip to London just to have his hair cut. Though Emma does not feel inclined to give up her vow to remain single, she decides that Frank is pleasing enough that she does not mind being associated with him in other people's minds. Mr. Knightley thinks Frank is a silly young man, just as he had suspected.

Meanwhile, an invitation from the Coles, successful tradespeople who live in Highbury, creates a conundrum for Emma. She had originally decided that she would not accept an invitation from the nouveau-riche family, but when everyone except the Woodhouses receives an invitation to a dinner party at the Coles' home, Emma feels left out. When an invitation arrives, she decides to accept it.

SUMMARY: CHAPTER 26

Emma arrives at the Coles' party behind Mr. Knightley. Because Knightley usually walks, Emma is surprised that he has come in his carriage. At dinner, it is revealed that Jane Fairfax has received the mysterious gift of a pianoforte. People assume the piano is from Colonel Campbell, but Emma tells Frank she suspects that it is a gift from Mr. Dixon. When Jane arrives later, she blushes when questioned about the piano.

Meanwhile, Mrs. Weston tells Emma that Mr. Knightley brought his carriage so that he could convey Jane home. Mrs. Weston suggests that a match may be forming between Jane and Mr. Knightley, but Emma resists this supposition vigorously, explaining that she cannot bear the thought of Mr. Knightley marrying because then her nephew, George and Isabella's son Henry, will not be able to inherit Donwell Abbey, the Knightley estate in the town of the same name. Mrs. Weston suspects that Mr. Knightley is the one who sent Jane the pianoforte.

Emma and Jane sing and play the piano for the company, with Frank accompanying. When Frank persuades Jane to sing one more song after her voice has begun to grow hoarse, Mr. Knightley intervenes. Emma questions Mr. Knightley about the carriage and pianoforte. His answers convince her that he did not send the gift, but do not enable her to decide if he has feelings for Jane. When impromptu dancing begins, she is relieved that he does not ask Jane to dance. Emma is also pleased that Frank immediately asks her and not Jane for a dance. There is time for only two dances, however, before the party breaks up. Frank comments to Emma that he is lucky the dancing had to end; otherwise he would have found himself asking Jane Fairfax for a dance.

SUMMARY: CHAPTER 27

Emma is thoroughly pleased with her evening at the Coles, but she is uncertain about the appropriateness of telling Frank about her suspicions about Jane or acknowledging the superiority of Jane's musical abilities. At the Coles' party, Harriet heard that Mr. Martin had dined with the Cox family, and there is a rumor that a Cox daughter would like to marry Mr. Martin. To distract and protect Harriet, Emma accompanies her on a shopping trip. They then decide to pay a visit to the Bates household and run into Frank and Mrs. Weston on their way. The visit seems to have been Frank's idea, but he offers to stay with Emma and send Mrs. Weston to make the visit on her own. Emma sends him along, knowing that he will later come see her at Hartfield, but Miss Bates then comes into the shop to ask Emma to come give her opinion of Jane's new pianoforte. In her rambling, Miss Bates reveals that Mr. Knightley has sent his last apples of the season to Jane, who is particularly fond of them.

ANALYSIS: CHAPTERS 25–27

Emma's indecision about whether to attend the Coles' dinner party brings the novel's complicated treatment of the issue of class to the fore. It is difficult for us, as modern-day, democratically minded readers, to agree with Austen's acceptance of the idea that class differences delineate real differences in intelligence and moral and emotional refinement. Yet Mr. Knightley's objection to a match between Harriet and Mr. Elton, because Harriet's unknown parentage means that she belongs to a lower class, makes it seem that Austen reinforces the class hierarchy. Throughout the novel, Knighley's reason and judgment stand in as surrogates for Austen's own, and whether or not she believes that class distinctions are always fair, Austen certainly does not aim to overturn the notion of class.

At the same time, Austen ridicules Emma's scrupulous and wavering decision about whether to refuse the Coles' invitation, emphasizing Emma's vanity. When the narrator tells us that Emma "regretted that her father's known habits would be giving her refusal less meaning than she could wish"—that Emma is worried that the Coles will think she has refused the invitation because her father is antisocial rather than because the Coles are beneath the Woodhouses—we see that Emma doesn't simply believe herself superior to the Coles. She mean-spiritedly desires to make the Coles feel slighted. The fact that both Mr. Weston and Mr. Knightley accept the Coles' invitation further reinforces the unreasonable nature of Emma's scruples.

In her evaluation of Frank Churchill, Emma shows her understanding of class to be truly superficial and dangerous. When Frank elegantly laughs off his folly in going to London for a haircut, Emma observes, "[S]illy things do cease to be silly if they are done by sensible people in an impudent way. Wickedness is always wickedness, but folly is not always folly. It depends upon the character of those who handle it." Frank does not seem to us the "sensible" person Emma tells herself he is, so we see that the real reason Emma excuses Frank's frivolous behavior is his elegant, charming manner—the result of his high-class upbringing. Finally, when Mr. Knightley meets Emma at the Coles', he mocks Emma's approving statement that his arrival by carriage befits a gentleman, saying, "How lucky that we should arrive at the same moment; for, if we had met first in the drawing-room, I doubt whether you would have discerned me to be more of a gentleman than usual." Knightley's comment highlights the fact that Emma does sometimes base her class consciousness on appearances but also that, for Emma's opinions of Knightley, their usual familiarity overrides this potentially dangerous way of looking at things.

CHAPTERS 28–30

SUMMARY: CHAPTER 28

Emma enters the Bates' sitting room and finds Frank occupied with fixing Mrs. Bates's glasses and Jane seated at the piano. Frank asks Jane questions about how she imagines the piano came to her, and his comment, "True affection only could have prompted it," makes Jane blush. Believing that Frank is teasing Jane unkindly about Mr. Dixon, Emma whispers that he should stop, and she regrets having shared her speculations about Jane with him. Mr. Knightley stops by to check on Jane's health but refuses to come in when he hears that Frank is there.

SUMMARY: CHAPTER 29

While the Woodhouses are visiting Randalls, Frank and Emma work on planning a ball so they can finish the dancing inaugurated at the Coles'. They decide the room at Randalls is too small. Mr. Woodhouse privately tells Mrs. Weston his concern that Frank is so thoughtless about opening and shutting doors that he exposes Emma, Harriet, and Mrs. Weston to dangerous drafts. The next solution proposed by Frank on behalf of Mr. Weston is that the ball be given at the Crown Inn. Though Frank does a poor job reassuring Mr. Woodhouse that this plan will not give them all colds, Emma comforts her father, and she agrees to the plan. There are further practical difficulties, and Frank proposes he go fetch Miss Bates along with her niece, whom Frank admits he does not immediately recollect, for advice. By the time he returns, the difficulties have been resolved, the date of the ball has been set, and Frank secures from Emma a promise to dance the first two dances with him.

SUMMARY: CHAPTER 30

Emma is worried that Frank's aunt, Mrs. Churchill, will refuse Frank permission to stay on for the ball, which is scheduled for a few days after his visit is scheduled to end. To everyone's relief, he receives this permission. Only Mr. Knightley refuses to look forward to the ball: he does not seem interested in dancing. Emma takes Knightley's diffidence as further proof that he is not interested in Jane, who in a rare moment of openness confesses how much she looks forward to the ball.

Two days later, Frank is called back to Enscombe because his aunt is ill. The ball is postponed indefinitely, and Frank comes to Emma to say goodbye. He is clearly dejected and speaks haltingly—for a moment, it seems as if he is going to declare something serious. Interrupted by his father, Frank departs, and Emma is depressed. Highbury society is, it seems for Emma, severely diminished without Frank's charms. Emma concludes that she must be "a little in love" with Frank after all.

ANALYSIS: CHAPTERS 28–30

During Emma and Frank's visit to the Bates', Emma, Frank, and Jane are all aware that the dialogue taking place has a subtext, but Austen crafts Frank's words so that the subtexts Emma and Jane read differ from one another. At this point in the novel, our misperceptions are likely to closely match Emma's, and we follow her in believing that Frank's teasing of Jane about the origins of her piano cruelly refers to Mr. Dixon.

Though Emma gossips maliciously about Jane, her selfless protectiveness of Jane when she believes Frank to be teasing her shows that Emma's willingness to amuse herself at the expense of another has limits. When we later learn that the piano is actually a gift from Frank, Jane's secret fiancé, we realize that his teasing is more good-natured, emphasizing his own gesture of affection.

Frank's request that Jane play one of the waltzes from the previous night's dance is similarly misinterpreted by Emma. He says:

> If you are very kind, [you will play] one of the waltzes we danced last night; let me live them over again. You did not enjoy them as I did; you appeared tired the whole time. I believe you were glad we danced no longer; I would have given worlds—all the worlds one ever has to give—for another half-hour.

As Frank's dance partner, Emma believes that Frank's directs his compliment toward her—that he implies to Jane that she did not enjoy the dancing because Emma and Frank were not dancing together. Once Frank's relationship with Jane is revealed, it becomes clear that that Frank would have given worlds for another half-hour not because he wished to dance more with Emma, but because he wanted the opportunity to ask Jane. When Jane complies with Frank's request by playing a tune that Frank recognizes as one that was danced at Weymouth, Jane flushes, and Emma assumes Jane is embarrassed because she had danced with Mr. Dixon to that song. In hindsight, it is clear that Frank was Jane's partner.

When Frank takes his leave of Emma before returning to Enscombe, our confusion about his feelings for Emma increases. After mentioning to Emma that he has already said goodbye to the Bateses and Jane, Frank hesitates, then says, "[P]erhaps, Miss Woodhouse—I think you can hardly be quite without suspicion—." This remark sounds to us, as it does to Emma, like the prelude to some sort of admission of love. Once we know Frank's true circumstances, though, it becomes clear that Frank is considering making Emma a genuine friend by letting her in on his and Jane's secret.

Emma's thoughts about Frank reveal to us that she is lying to herself about loving him; she only enjoys the attention Frank's courtship brings her. She takes pleasure in dancing with him because

everyone else admires what a fine couple they are, not because the
two share any intimacy. She is excited with the prospect of seeing
him each day because she knows that he admires her and because
she suspects that he harbors feelings for her. She misses his company
because it has enlivened Highbury, but she does not miss him as a
person. At the conclusion of Chapter 30, Emma's attempt to convince herself that she loves Frank—"I must be in love; I should be
the oddest creature in the world if I were not—for a few weeks at
least"—shows us that Emma does not (yet) truly understand what
love feels like.

CHAPTERS 31–33

SUMMARY: CHAPTER 31
Emma imagines the course that her and Frank's love affair will run.
In her mind, her fantasy always ends with her refusing Frank. She
believes she loves him, but not so much that her happiness depends
upon him, and that he loves her, but that his feelings are probably
changeable. She reads his first letter to Mrs. Weston after returning
to Enscombe and admires the genuineness of the warm feelings
Frank expresses for Highbury. His brief mention of Harriet makes
Emma speculate that Harriet could replace her in his affections, but
she reaffirms her resolution to cease matchmaking.

Village gossip turns to Mr. Elton, who will soon arrive in Highbury with his new bride. Harriet is flustered by the prospect of
Elton's return, and Emma suggests that if Harriet will not forget
Elton for her own sake, she should do so for Emma's, for Harriet's
persistent attachment is a reminder of Emma's guilt. Harriet
repents, and Emma is moved by the warmth of Harriet's love for her.
Emma concludes that tenderness of heart, which Harriet possesses
and which Emma believes she herself lacks, is tremendously valuable.

SUMMARY: CHAPTER 32
Mr. Elton returns with his bride, and Emma decides that she and
Harriet should visit the newlyweds early on in order to reestablish
normal social relations. In this first meeting and shortly thereafter
Emma reserves judgment on Mrs. Elton, and attributes Mr. Elton's
lack of ease to the awkwardness of the situation. When the couple
returns the visit and comes to Hartfield, Emma is able to observe
Mrs. Elton at greater length, and Emma is horrified by the over-

familiarity of her manners. Mrs. Elton is attached to superficial tokens of wealth, such as her sister and brother-in-law's "barouche-landau" (carriage); she presumes to take Emma under her social wing; and she prides herself on the inner "resources" of self-worth and foresight that she clearly lacks. Mr. Woodhouse, never particularly discerning, considers the new bride pleasant enough and expresses guilt that he has not visited her. He cannot understand Emma's consternation when he suggests that "[a] bride, you know, my dear, is always the first in company," and that a bride receives the utmost in politeness and good manners.

SUMMARY: CHAPTER 33
Emma continues to dislike Mrs. Elton, who, noting Emma's reserve, begins to return the sentiment. Emma assumes that Mr. Elton has told his wife something of the unfortunate episode with her and Harriet, to whom the Eltons are especially rude. Mrs. Elton takes on Jane Fairfax as her project, attempting to bring her out socially. Emma is puzzled that Jane refuses another invitation to join Mr. and Mrs. Campbell and Mr. and Mrs. Dixon in Ireland. She is also puzzled that Jane accepts Mrs. Elton's attentions, and she discusses Jane's actions with Mrs. Weston and Mr. Knightley. Mr. Knightley defends Jane's acceptance of Mrs. Elton's attentions, and Emma takes the opportunity to probe Mr. Knightley on his feelings for Jane, telling him, "The extent of your admiration may take you by surprise one day or other." Knightley seems flustered, uneasy, and embarrassed and wonders whether Emma has been playing matchmaker for him. She assures him that she has not, and he insists her that he is not in love with Jane—for one thing, Jane is too reserved. Emma is satisfied that she has been right about Knightley's feelings for Jane and that Mrs. Weston has been wrong, but Mrs. Weston wonders if his eagerness in denying it indicates otherwise.

ANALYSIS: CHAPTERS 31–33
In these chapters, Emma's imaginative preoccupations again shift their focus from meddling in others' lives to understanding the intrigue in her own. Earlier in the novel, Emma occupies herself by envisaging Jane Fairfax's supposed affair with Mr. Dixon, but Jane's reserve and Emma's growing compassion for her have made this line of speculation less worthwhile for Emma; now, for the first time in the novel, Emma imagines herself as the heroine of her own plot. Even so, her sentiments for Frank Churchill are no more real than

the feelings that she wrongly attributes to Mr. Elton, Jane, and Mr. Knightley. Notably, her feelings for Frank flourish only in his absence, which leaves Emma not unhappy but "busy and cheerful." She relishes the chance to envision her and Frank's courtship, picturing "a thousand amusing schemes for the progress and close of their attachment, fancying interesting dialogues, and inventing elegant letters." She does not seem to relish the prospect of a courtship itself.

Meanwhile, Mrs. Elton seems like a crude parody of the earlier Emma, exhibiting Emma's mistakes in an exaggerated form. Mrs. Elton is constantly in search of young women to whom she can attach herself and introduce into her society, and she holds matchmaking an important goal. Emma immediately resents Mrs. Elton's presumptuousness in thinking she can make matches between strangers, and Mrs. Elton's blunt, outspoken nature makes us share Emma's resentment. Still, no great difference exists between Mrs. Elton's behavior toward Jane and Emma's behavior toward Harriet, though Emma herself cannot recognize the similarity. Both Emma and Mrs. Elton are guilty of presumption.

The conversation Emma and Mrs. Weston have with Knightley presents another example of a dialogue with a subtext that can be understood only upon a second reading of the novel. Knightley is obviously uncomfortable when Emma suggests that he has feelings for Jane, and his uneasy reaction could be interpreted a number of ways. Knightley may flush simply because he resents personal questions, or because, as Mrs. Weston suspects, he is fighting or concealing his feelings for Jane. We suspect that he flushes because he is displeased that Emma so blithely imagines him with someone else, and he seems relieved when she assures him that this has not been the case. Mrs. Weston's willingness to read between the lines and have faith in Knightley's refutation at the end of the chapter reinforces the novel's message that seeking subtexts can alert one to a hidden truth but can just as easily lead one into error.

CHAPTERS 34–36

SUMMARY: CHAPTER 34

Fulfilling a social obligation, Emma plans a dinner party for Mrs. Elton. Harriet asks to be excused from attending, which gives Emma the opportunity to ease her conscience regarding Jane Fairfax, who, at Harriet's announced absence, is promptly invited to fill the empty eighth seat. Mr. John Knightley is also included because he will be in Highbury, accompanying his two eldest sons on a visit to their aunt and grandfather.

At the party, Mr. John Knightley gently reproaches Jane for fetching letters from the post office that morning in the rain. Jane acts as if the situation is not a big deal but ends up blushing and watery-eyed, and soon the rest of the party begins discussing the matter. Mrs. Elton insists that her servant should be given the task of retrieving Jane's letters, and Jane firmly resists. The conversation moves to handwriting. Mr. Knightley praises Emma's penmanship but dissents when she praises the penmanship of Frank Churchill. Jane's eagerness to fetch her own letters rouses Emma's suspicions, but she decides not to trouble Jane by questioning her.

Summary: Chapter 35

The women gather in the drawing room after dinner, and Mrs. Elton pursues the subject of letter-retrieval with Jane. She also insists on helping Jane find a governess position, though Jane explains that she will not seek a place until after she sees the Campbells in mid-summer. The men come in, and Mr. Weston, who has been on business in London, appears. He brings a letter from Frank, reporting that Mrs. Churchill has decided that the household should make an extended visit in London. This news means that Frank will be able to be in Highbury a good deal. Mr. and Mrs. Weston are pleased, Emma is somewhat agitated, and Mr. Knightley seems unexcited by the news.

Summary: Chapter 36

Mr. Weston and Mrs. Elton have a long-winded conversation in which they pursue comically different purposes. Mrs. Elton fishes for compliments and goes on about Maple Grove, the estate where her wealthy brother and sister-in-law live. Mr. Weston talks about Frank and explains the illness of Frank's aunt (and Mr. Weston's sister-in-law), Mrs. Churchill. Before the conversation becomes too heated, they are interrupted by tea. Mr. John Knightley gives Emma final instructions regarding his sons and wonders if they will be in the way at Hartfield, now that Emma has become so social. She rejects John Knightley's implication and insists that she is more of a homebody than Mr. (George) Knightley, who seems pleased and amused by the assertion.

ANALYSIS: CHAPTERS 34–36

Austen's use of three chapters to narrate a single dinner party marks an interesting narrative development for English literature. In novels by previous writers, the description of the events of a dinner party would have taken up at most a page or two, but Austen turns the dinner party into an opportunity to trace extensively the ins and outs of human personality and interaction. In doing so, she provides a model for later writers as disparate as Henry James and Virginia Woolf.

During the dinner party, we are given our first extended view of Jane Fairfax, who begins to come out of her reserved shell and speak more. Her well-crafted comments exemplify an ideal balance between openness and propriety. For example, when Mr. John Knightley observes, "When you have lived to my age, you will begin to think letters are never worth going through the rain for," Jane answers, "I must not hope to be ever situated as you are, in the midst of every dearest connection, and therefore I cannot expect that simply growing older should make me indifferent about letters." This answer is politely vague but also expresses real emotion. It engages our pity, but it tactfully avoids any suggestion of self-pity on Jane's part. Furthermore, when she firmly resists Mrs. Elton's aggressive offers of assistance, we realize that Jane's quietness and reserve do not indicate that she is dull or passive—she clearly has a mind of her own. In fact, Jane is the character who voices the novel's most explicit social protest, which seems to come directly from Austen herself. Jane speaks against the "governess-trade," which involves "the sale, not quite of human flesh, but of human intellect." She admits that offices that advertise for governess positions are less morally deplorable than slave traders, but she adds, "[B]ut as to the greater misery of the victims, I do not know where it lies."

Our experience of the dinner party is also enlivened by Austen's depiction of the absurdity that often characterizes forced social dialogue. The conversation between Mrs. Elton and Mr. Weston is full of ridiculous, discontinuous shifts of topic. Mrs. Elton continually turns the conversation to the topic of herself and her relations, and Mr. Weston is every bit as determined to turn the conversation back to his son, at one point jumping in when Mrs. Elton is interrupted by a coughing fit. Mrs. Elton's affected airs are completely lost on Mr. Weston—when she protests that her sister is "no fine lady," she means that her sister is not overly fussy, but Mr. Weston takes her quite literally. Mrs. Elton's affected speech and her tactic of fishing for compliments reinforces our sense of her superficiality, while Mr. Weston's remarks suggest that there is something a little automatic and absentminded in his perpetual sociability.

CHAPTERS 37–39

SUMMARY: CHAPTER 37
Emma thinks about her agitation upon hearing of Frank's impending arrival and decides that she feels such apprehension more on his behalf than her own—her attachment to him is not very strong. When she sees him again, he is friendly and spirited but visits for only fifteen minutes. Frank's short visit convinces Emma that his feelings as well must have weakened. Because of his aunt's demands, Frank is kept away for ten days after this first visit. Mrs. Churchill eventually determines that her family must move from London to Richmond, which places Frank closer to Highbury. Mr. Weston is delighted to have his son nearer, and a date is set for the long-postponed ball.

SUMMARY: CHAPTER 38
The day of the ball arrives. Emma is invited by Mr. Weston to come early and give her opinion on the arrangements, and she believes that this opportunity will give some privacy to her second meeting with Frank, who will be with his father. But Emma is not the only one of Mr. Weston's "favourites" that he has entreated to come early, and all the while Frank seems excited but restless, constantly moving to see who has arrived. Finally, when Jane and Miss Bates arrive, Frank rushes out to help them with umbrellas. Mrs. Elton pronounces Frank a very fine young man. Miss Bates overwhelms everyone with exclamations of gratitude and pleasure. Frank tells Emma that he dislikes Mrs. Elton and her familiar manner with Jane, and he runs off again to ask his father when the dancing will begin.

Mr. and Mrs. Weston suddenly realize that Mrs. Elton expects to be asked to lead the dance and that they cannot give Emma that honor, as they had hoped. Despite this slight disappointment, Emma enjoys the beginning of the festivities, though she is disturbed that Mr. Knightley will not dance. She admires the figure he cuts among the other men, and he notices that he is watching her. The ball is a success, and only one episode mars Emma's enjoyment. During one dance, Harriet is left without a partner, and Mr. Elton, the one dancer who is disengaged, pointedly refuses to ask her. Mr. Knightley soothes Harriet's embarrassment by asking her to dance, and Emma is very pleased with him. Later, she expresses her gratitude, and he asks her why the Eltons are her enemies. She admits that she wanted Mr. Elton to marry Harriet and acknowledges that Knightley was right about his character. Knightley in return admits that Harriet has more admirable qualities than he originally thought. Emma and Knightley cement their new mutual understanding with a dance.

SUMMARY: CHAPTER 39

Emma looks back on her talk with Mr. Knightley at the ball with pleasure, and she rejoices that the Eltons' rudeness has cured Harriet of her infatuation with Mr. Elton. Suddenly, Frank appears with Harriet, fainting, on his arm. When revived, Harriet tells the story of how she was walking with a friend, Miss Bickerton, when a Gypsy child approached to beg from them. Miss Bickerton, frightened, ran away, but Harriet was unable to follow because of a cramp she had gotten at the ball. Just as she started to panic, a group of Gypsies surrounded her and demanded money. Frank happened to be walking along and frightened the Gypsies away. Emma cannot help but wonder whether this romantic circumstance might make Harriet and Frank interesting to each other. The episode alarms Mr. Woodhouse and is occasion for gossip, but the Gypsies leave the neighborhood and no harm is done.

ANALYSIS: CHAPTERS 37–39

Emma's honest reflections about her lack of substantive feelings for Frank reveal her growing maturity. She no longer sees him as a character in the scenes she imagines for herself, someone who is important simply because he gives her the opportunity to show off her accomplishments and elegance. She recognizes that if their two-month separation has not cooled his love, "there were dangers and evils before her: caution for him and for herself would be necessary." Rather than anticipating a dramatic scene, she now hopes that "she might be able to keep him from an absolute declaration. That would be so very painful a conclusion of their present acquaintance." Emma's decision to observe Frank to see how he feels, rather than to begin with an assumption about how he feels, enables her to understand that Frank is not in love with her. The narrator makes clear that Emma's vanity is not at issue in this case—she is relieved, not offended, that Frank's feelings are cooled, and at the dance, she seems to find more interest in puzzling about his odd mood than in courting his attention. When Frank and Emma dance, instead of imagining how elegant they look to others, she admires how elegant Mr. Knightley looks. Emma has become more concerned with observing others, and less concerned with being observed by others.

The Gypsies Harriet describes encountering in Chapter 39 seem a strange intrusion into the domestic realism of the story. It is almost as if they have wandered in from a different novel entirely. In the episode, Austen plays with the conventions of romantic melodrama, one of which was the rescue of a "damsel in distress" as the beginning to a romantic relationship. Yet, in the calculating context established by the novel, the encounter seems to predict a lack of destiny rather than a fated match. The improbability of Harriet's encounter with Frank alerts us to the improbability of their ending up together. We can see that the extraordinary circumstances that have thrown Harriet and Frank together owe nothing to their shared values or qualities—a chance meeting and rescue present no evidence that the two belong together. And while Harriet's passivity is in keeping with the conventions of a romance, it is not something that we would expect Austen's novel to reward. The happiest women in the novel are not weak and passive, but both mentally and physically vigorous.

Emma's willingness to accept the improbability of Harriet's encounter with Frank as proof that there must be some sort of connection between the two indicates that her fancy has not been entirely cured of its tendency toward ungrounded speculation. Emma may be learning to place Mr. Knightley's approval of her more recent actions above Frank Churchill's charms, but she has a few more lessons to learn before she gains a full understanding of herself.

CHAPTERS 40–42

SUMMARY: CHAPTER 40

Harriet comes to tell Emma that her infatuation with Mr. Elton has passed and to relinquish the trinkets she has kept to remember him by. First, she shows Emma a bit of court-plaster (used at the time as a bandage) that she had lent to Mr. Elton when he cut himself. He had used what he needed but discarded the rest, which Harriet then kept. Emma feels guilty in recalling that she had lied and said that she did not have any court-plaster, so that Harriet would have the opportunity to be Elton's healer. Harriet's second trinket is a useless bit of pencil Elton had discarded. She throws both items into the fire, and Emma hopes that Frank might take Elton's place. Her hopes seem to be rewarded when, during another conversation, Harriet says she will never marry, inciting Emma's suspicion that Harriet does not think that she will marry because she is interested in someone of a higher class. After some hesitation, Emma asks if Harriet has feelings for someone of higher rank. Harriet says yes, and Emma comments that she is not surprised, given the service that this person rendered Harriet. Emma says that they must not discuss it anymore, and she advises Harriet to be cautious but not to give up all hope.

SUMMARY: CHAPTER 41

Mr. Knightley begins to suspect that there is some secret understanding between Frank and Jane. During a walk with Emma, Harriet, Mr. and Mrs. Weston, Frank, Jane, and Miss Bates, Knightley witnesses a strange exchange. Frank asks Mrs. Weston if anything has come of Mr. Perry's plan to buy a carriage. She has no idea what he is talking about, and he swears that she wrote of it in a letter to him some months ago. She denies it, and Frank decides he must have dreamed it. Miss Bates remembers that there was talk of the Perrys getting a carriage at her house (with Jane present) but that it was a secret. Mr. Knightley observes Frank trying to catch Jane's eye after this.

The party reaches Hartfield, and Emma persuades everyone to come in for tea. A word game ensues, which Mr. Knightley watches. Frank constructs the word "blunder" using alphabet tiles, which he shows to Jane. Then he constructs the word "Dixon," shows it to Emma, who laughs, and then shows it to Jane, who pushes the puzzle away in anger. When the party breaks up, Knightley stays behind to speak to Emma—he knows that everyone considers her the object of Frank's affection, and he wishes to warn her. Knightley asks Emma about the "Dixon" joke, and, embarrassed, she refuses to explain. He tells her his suspicion about Jane and Frank, and she laughs at him, stating unequivocally that she can answer for Frank's indifference to Jane. Knightley is silenced and irritated by Emma's implication that she is in Frank's confidence.

SUMMARY: CHAPTER 42

An outing to Box Hill is planned, but it has to be postponed because of a lame horse. Mr. Knightley half-jokingly suggests that the party come to his estate instead. Mrs. Elton seizes upon the idea, and Knightley has to be firm to prevent her from planning all the details. Meanwhile, the lame horse heals, and it is decided that the Box Hill party will follow the one at Donwell Abbey, Knightley's estate. At Donwell Abbey, Emma enjoys examining Knightley's house and grounds. She overhears Jane resisting a governess "situation" that Mrs. Elton has found for her. Walking through the garden, Emma finds Harriet and Knightley looking out over the Martin family home and thinks the two an odd grouping, but is nevertheless convinced that Harriet is in good hands. Mrs. Weston is worried by the fact that Frank is late coming from Richmond. At the house, Emma encounters an agitated Jane, who asks her to tell everyone else that she has walked home. Frank then turns up out of humor and in the course of conversation says that he would like to go abroad. Emma teases him out of his mood, and he promises to join the Box Hill trip.

ANALYSIS: CHAPTERS 40–42

Even though Emma has resolved to use more discretion in promoting a match between Harriet and Frank than she used when encouraging Harriet's affection for Mr. Elton, she manages to cause a misunderstanding precisely because she shies away from explicit statements. When Emma says of Harriet's new object of affection, "The service he rendered you was enough to warm your heart," she is referring to Frank, who saved Harriet from the Gypsies. Harriet, however, thinks of Mr. Knightley, who saved her from humiliation by asking her to dance.

In the way it keeps us in the dark about the truth of various characters' feelings, *Emma* reads like a detective novel. The picnic presents subtle mysteries: Jane's agitation is not explained, nor is Frank's sudden ill temper. We suspect that Jane's and Frank's bad moods must be linked, but Austen keeps us in suspense as to what exactly has transpired. Even straightforward Mr. Knightley is drawn into the atmosphere of speculation when he suggests that Jane and Frank have been corresponding throughout Frank's absence. Also, Knightley wrongly takes Emma's statement that Frank has no feelings for Jane as a suggestion that Frank and Emma have some sort of romantic association. In truth, Emma's confidence is purely the result of the unflattering things Frank has said to her about Jane.

The word game the party plays in Chapter 41 functions as a metaphor for all the games of private concealment and revelation that characterize Highbury society. Emma and Mr. Knightley are both able to decode the words that Frank makes, but, because they possess different kinds of information, they interpret these words differently. Knightley understands that the word "blunder" must refer to Frank's misplaced question to Mrs. Weston about Mr. Perry's carriage, a message that Emma is unable to decode. Emma interprets "Dixon" as a cruel joke on Jane, but Knightley rightly understands that Frank's presentation of the word to Jane is a mark of some intimacy between them. When Knightley observes to himself, "These letters were but the vehicle for gallantry and trick. It was a child's play, chosen to conceal a deeper game on Frank Churchill's part," he makes explicit the novel's suggestion that social intercourse is a game with particular rules. Like a game, social interaction requires skill and sometimes produces winners and losers.

Although the narrator typically describes all events from Emma's point of view, Chapter 41 is unique in that it is narrated entirely from Mr. Knightley's point of view, depending on what he can see of the word games transpiring in the parlor. By shifting to Mr. Knightley's point of view, we get a new perspective on the mixture of knowledge and bewilderment that each character experiences. This new emphasis on Mr. Knightley's character and point of view subtly alerts us that he is becoming a central character.

CHAPTERS 43–45

SUMMARY: CHAPTER 43

> *How could she have been so brutal ... to Miss Bates! ... And how suffer him to leave her without saying one word of common kindness!*
> *(See* QUOTATIONS, *p. 67)*

The Box Hill trip is not a success. Mr. and Mrs. Elton keep to themselves; Mr. Knightley, Miss Bates, and Jane form a second exclusive party; and Emma stays with Harriet and Frank. Emma is disappointed by Harriet's and Frank's dullness. Later, Frank becomes excessively lively and gallant. Emma is confident that there is nothing behind his flirtations, but she is aware that others can pick up on their flirtation. The party sits about listlessly, and Frank says that Emma demands to know what they are thinking of. Mrs. Elton is offended by Frank's deference to Emma, and Knightley asks dryly if she would *really* like to know what he is thinking. Frank then demands a piece of cleverness from each member of the party, asking them to produce either "one thing very clever . . . or two things moderately clever; or three things very dull indeed." Miss Bates good-naturedly comments that the she will have no trouble meeting the last requirement, but Emma responds, "Ah! ma'am, but there may be a difficulty. Pardon me, but you will be limited as to number—only three at once." Mr. Weston offers a conundrum in praise of Emma, and the Eltons leave in disgust for a walk.

Frank comments that sometimes matches made in public places become regrettable on further acquaintance and that, as a result, Mr. and Mrs. Elton are lucky that they are compatible. Jane demurs and leaves for a walk with her aunt and Mr. Knightley. Emma, left with Frank, grows tired of his flattery. Later, Mr. Knightley takes Emma aside and reprimands her for her conduct toward Miss Bates, reminding Emma that Miss Bates has had an unfortunate life and deserves compassion. Emma has never felt "so agitated, so mortified, [so] grieved" in her life; she cries almost all the way home.

SUMMARY: CHAPTER 44
On reflection, Emma decides that the Box Hill party was a disaster. Still feeling horrible about her treatment of Miss Bates, Emma soothes her conscience by visiting the Bateses first thing the following morning. Miss Bates's humility and kindness are a further reproach to Emma's bad behavior. During Emma's visit, Jane remains in the bedroom with a headache.

Jane has just accepted the governess position recommended by Mrs. Elton, and Emma expresses surprise and genuine concern for the unhappiness Jane's departure must cause everyone. Jane will leave within a fortnight (two weeks). Emma is surprised to learn that Frank departed the previous evening for Richmond, and she is struck by the difference between Mrs. Churchill's power and Jane's. She is ashamed of her earlier conjectures about Jane's relationship with Mr. Dixon.

SUMMARY: CHAPTER 45
Emma returns to Hartfield to discover that Mr. Knightley and Harriet have arrived in her absence. Knightley is about to depart for London to visit John and Isabella. His hastiness surprises Emma.

Mr. Woodhouse inquires about Emma's visit with the Bateses, and Emma blushes and exchanges a glance with Knightley. She believes he understands her feelings and forgives her. He makes an unusual gesture, taking her hand and almost kissing it. She is gratified, though a little puzzled about his scruple in completing the kiss.

The next day, unexpected news arrives: Mrs. Churchill has died. Emma thinks this event may improve Harriet's chances with Frank. Meanwhile, she attempts to provide assistance to Jane, inviting her to Hartfield, sending her healthful foods, and attempting to visit her. Jane pleads ill health, but Emma hears that Jane has been taking outside exercise, and she feels hurt that Jane seems to be particularly avoiding her.

ANALYSIS: CHAPTERS 43–45

In *Emma*, Austen presents cleverness as a generally favorable attribute by making it one of her protagonist's admirable qualities. Austen's depiction of cleverness was not so kind in previous novels, however. In *Mansfield Park*, the novel Austen wrote before *Emma*, the heroine is unfailingly earnest and good, and her main adversary is a woman who is clever and superficial, implying that cleverness is a dangerous quality, not one to be confused with virtue.

Though cleverness is depicted favorably in general in *Emma*, the Box Hill scene presents cleverness as a hurtful force. Frank Churchill's ability to deceive everyone into believing he is infatuated with Emma is powered by his restless frustration. Fortunately, Emma is sensible enough not to be taken in by his flirtations, but a less perceptive woman might have been hurt when she discovered they were not serious. Moreover, Frank's attentions, and Emma's acceptance of them, cause pain to Mr. Knightley, and we later realize that Frank's flirting with Emma is also hurtful to Jane.

Emma's hurtful response to Miss Bates in Chapter 43 is the most blatant example of cleverness as a harmful quality and a clear sign that Frank's lack of seriousness has had a bad effect on Emma. In tone and substance, Emma's sarcastic remark to Miss Bates squarely hits its target, but it displays a casual cruelty that we have never seen in Emma before. Mr. Knightley's reprimand and Emma's subsequent chagrin may qualify as the greatest emotional crisis in the novel—it is certainly the crisis that is described with the most directness and at the greatest length. Unlike Emma's unpleasant surprise regarding Mr. Elton and the emotional fluctuations that have accompanied her experiences with Frank, Knightley's disapproval drives Emma to tears.

When Mr. Knightley reminds Emma that Miss Bates "is poor; she has sunk from the comforts she was born to; and if she live to old age must probably sink more," he reveals the harsh realities faced by single women in Austen's time. Genteel women who were not able to marry and who did not inherit enough wealth to support themselves were threatened not only with a loss of social privilege, but also with a fall in material comforts. Or, as in Jane Fairfax's case, they were forced into a kind of work that amounts to an almost complete loss of freedom. Emma is protected from this threat by her father's wealth, but we and Emma become increasingly aware that other women in Emma's society are not so lucky.

CHAPTERS 46–48

SUMMARY: CHAPTER 46

Mr. Weston arrives to escort Emma to see Mrs. Weston—clearly something is amiss. Assured that Mrs. Weston is well, Emma's first concern is for Isabella's family and for Mr. Knightley in London, but Mr. Weston assures her that the news does not involve them. At Randalls, Emma is greeted by Mrs. Weston, who explains that Frank has just revealed that he and Jane have been secretly engaged. Emma is shocked, embarrassed by the things she has said to Frank about Jane, and concerned for Harriet's feelings.

Emma quickly relieves Mrs. Weston by assuring her that she has no feelings for Frank. She is angry, however, about his behavior toward her and Jane. Mrs. Weston defends her stepson, telling Emma that there were misunderstandings between him and Jane and that he will be writing her a letter detailing the extenuating circumstances. Mr. Churchill has given his consent to the match, though he has requested that it remain secret until more time has passed after his wife's death. Mr. Weston enters the room, and Emma assures him that the news of Frank's engagement has not caused her any pain.

SUMMARY: CHAPTER 47

> It darted through her with the speed of an arrow that
> Mr. Knightley must marry no one but herself!
>
> (See QUOTATIONS, p. 67)

Emma is filled with concern for Harriet. She is angrier at herself than she is at Frank, because she believes that she should have discouraged Harriet's attachment to him. Jane's behavior since her arrival in Highbury is also put into perspective. Emma realizes that Jane has been avoiding her because she has seen her as a rival. Emma dreads telling Harriet the news, but when Harriet arrives at Hartfield she has already heard the story from Mr. Weston. Emma is surprised at Harriet's composure, and it turns out that Harriet never cared for Frank; she has been harboring feelings for Mr. Knightley. Harriet knows that Mr. Knightley is of higher rank than she, but she affirms that Emma has given her hope that she may raise herself enough to be acceptable to him.

Emma makes a startling discovery—she herself is in love with Mr. Knightley! She conceals her emotion from Harriet, asking Harriet whether she has reason to believe that Knightley returns her feelings. Harriet recounts a number of instances in which Knightley has shown her special attention, many of which Emma's memory corroborates. When Harriet departs, Emma is left to reflect that she has been wrong about everything, including her own heart. Now Knightley may debase himself by marrying Harriet, and she has made it all possible.

SUMMARY: CHAPTER 48

Emma rethinks all of the events of the past months. She realizes that it has always been important to her to be "first" with Mr. Knightley and that he has always had special concern for her, but she cannot believe he could return her feelings, especially when he has just been so angry with her about her rudeness to Miss Bates. She still believes she would not marry him, even if he asked, because she cannot leave her father. She anticipates having the opportunity to observe him and Harriet together.

Mrs. Weston arrives to report that she has just visited with Jane and that Jane admitted to having suffered a good deal since entering into the secret engagement. She blames herself for her misjudgment and acknowledges Emma's kindness during her sickness. Hearing this account, Emma again expresses anger at Frank's behavior. Mrs. Weston again defends him, though she has not yet received his explanatory letter, but Emma is too distracted by her thoughts about Mr. Knightley to pay attention. Emma regrets once more that she was not a better friend to Jane, as Knightley had advised, and she reflects on how desolate life will be without Knightley's constant visits to Hartfield.

ANALYSIS: CHAPTERS 46–48

The novel's narrative pace speeds up in these chapters, as instead of facing a slow accumulation of details that require interpretation, we begin to be given the key detail for interpreting all that has transpired thus far—the answer to the question of who is in love with whom.

Austen's narrator finally describes Emma's development explicitly, rather than implicitly, as she does throughout the novel. At the same time, Harriet finally realizes Emma's limitations. Harriet begins her conversation with Emma about her feelings for Knightley with an assertion that Emma can "see into everybody's heart," but she soon understands that she has been wrong. Rather than waiting for Emma's approval of a match between herself and Knightley, Harriet proceeds to explain in a self-confident manner why she believes their disparity in rank need not be a hindrance. She goes so far as to express hope that Emma will not present obstacles to the match, demonstrating that her attachment to Knightley is stronger than her loyalty to her friend. When Emma asks whether Harriet has reasons to believe that her feelings are returned, Harriet answers "modestly, but not fearfully" in the affirmative.

The brief, general way in which the narrator describes Emma's realization of her love for Knightley makes Emma's previous inability to discover the truth about her feelings seem almost ridiculous.

> A few minutes were sufficient for making her acquainted with her own heart. A mind like hers, once opening to suspicion, made rapid progress; she touched, she admitted, she acknowledged the whole truth . . . Mr. Knightley must marry no one but herself!

As with Emma's emotional confrontation with Mr. Elton in Chapter 15, Austen shies away from describing in too much detail the shock of Emma's realization. Instead, the narrator moves on to Emma's reflections regarding her own conduct. The novel seems more comfortable making fine distinctions between social obligations and moral duties than in describing human passion directly. But perhaps the picture we have been given of the small gestures that continually pass between Emma and Mr. Knightley communicate their feelings more strongly than any direct description could.

There is something disturbing about the nature of Emma's realization that she has treated Harriet badly. Using free association to relate Emma's thoughts, the narrator comments, "She saw it all with a clearness which had never blessed her before. How improperly had she been acting by Harriet! How inconsiderate, how indelicate, how irrational, how unfeeling, had been her conduct!" Yet, following her mistake with Mr. Elton, Emma has already recognized the inappropriateness of meddling with Harriet's romantic life, and she has adjusted her behavior accordingly. Furthermore, Harriet now seems to have achieved the success Emma wished for her—a match with Knightley would raise her position in the world immensely. It is clear that Emma believes she has done wrong not because she has injured Harriet, but because she has injured herself, and possibly Mr. Knightley (by exposing him to an undignified match).

CHAPTERS 49–51

SUMMARY: CHAPTER 49

Seldom, very seldom does complete truth belong to any human disclosure; seldom can it happen that something is not a little disguised....

(See QUOTATIONS, *p. 68)*

Emma goes for a walk in the garden. To her surprise, Mr. Knightley joins her. He has just returned from London. She worries that Knightley will confess his feelings for Harriet, and she offers her news about Frank and Jane's secret engagement. Knightley already knows about it and offers his consolation, but Emma assures him she has never had feelings for Frank. She explains and expresses regret for her behavior, and Knightley is strangely silent. Finally, he admits he may have underrated Frank and expresses envy at his circumstances. Worried that Knightley is about to discuss Harriet, Emma quickly silences him. He is mortified, and seeing his pain Emma invites him to speak after all, saying she will be glad to hear him as a friend. He says he does not wish her friendship and declares his love. She is surprised, thrilled, and by the time they reach the house they are engaged to marry. Knightley is surprised as well—he was convinced that Emma was in love with Frank; he departed for London to cool his feelings for her, and he has returned thinking she would need comfort. He has moved from resigned despair to perfect happiness in half an hour.

SUMMARY: CHAPTER 50

Emma can barely conceal her feelings as she and Mr. Knightley join her father for tea. That night, Emma lies awake worrying about Harriet and her father. She decides she will write a letter to Harriet explaining what has happened and arrange for Harriet to visit Isabella in London to give both of them some time to adjust to the new situation. She decides that she and Knightley must postpone their wedding until after her father dies.

Mrs. Weston forwards Emma a letter from Frank in which he explains that all of his actions, including his attentions to Emma, were guided by a need to maintain the secrecy of his engagement to Jane. He apologizes for his behavior, but explains that he could tell Emma was not attached to him, and says that he was under the impression that Emma already knew about him and Jane. He adores Jane and is miserable that he has made her suffer. The couple quarreled the morning of the Donwell Abbey party because Jane was upset about his behavior toward Emma, thinking it an inappropriate way to maintain their secret. Frank was upset about Jane's caution, which he interpreted as coldness. Frank then left for Richmond, and Jane wrote to him to break off the engagement. He received the letter from Jane the morning his aunt died, and in the flurry of subsequent correspondence failed to send his conciliating response to her. She sent his letters back to him, indicating that he could return her letters at her governess post. This was the first news Frank had heard of her new position, and he threw himself at his uncle's mercy, receiving approval for the match. He then sped to Highbury to find Jane very ill. They reconciled, and Frank admits that he is happier than he deserves to be.

SUMMARY: CHAPTER 51

Emma, in her own happiness, cannot help but forgive Frank. When Knightley comes to her, she shares the letter with him. He reads the letter, telling Emma his impressions as he goes along, and he is less softened than she but willing to admit that Frank has some good qualities. He and Emma discuss her father, and he agrees that Emma cannot leave Hartfield and that Mr. Woodhouse cannot be expected to move to Donwell Abbey. He suggests that he move to Hartfield, and Emma is moved by his sacrifice. She promises to think it over, and soon likes the plan—her only sadness is that this engagement and relocation will estrange her and Harriet further.

ANALYSIS: CHAPTERS 49–51

Nearly every sentence that passes between Emma and Knightley in Chapter 49 is misinterpreted, reinforcing the picture the novel has given us of the difficulty of correctly interpreting social exchanges. Emma is reserved because she fears that Knightley will confide his attachment to Harriet, but Knightley mistakes Emma's reserve for grief at the loss of Frank. He also mistakes Emma's flush, when he says that he knows already about Frank and Jane, for suppressed unhappiness, when in truth Emma is worried that Knightley's knowledge of the situation comes from Harriet. When Emma congratulates Knightley on his insight into their relationship and sighs, "I seem to have been doomed to blindness," Knightley believes Emma is expressing her regret for having been attached to Frank, while Emma actually refers to her blindness with regard to Knightley himself.

The emotional release of Chapter 49 owes to both Knightley and Emma removing the restraints of verbal carefulness and propriety. Emma's forthright statement about her lack of feelings for Frank encourages Knightley, though he expects opposition and doubts whether his words are appropriate, to confess his feelings for Emma.

Mr. Knightley's declaration of his love to Emma contrasts starkly with Mr. Elton's elaborate compliments and with Frank's light, playful flirtations. Knightley says, "I cannot make speeches, Emma. . . . If I loved you less, I might be able to talk about it more. But you know what I am. You hear nothing but truth from me.... Yes, you see, you understand my feelings." One of the novel's messages is that such sincere, direct expressions are more valuable than ornate speech. The narrator's indirect description of Emma's response to Knightley—"She spoke then, on being so entreated. What did she say? Just what she ought, of course"—embodies the idea that often the truest feelings are best expressed through simple speech. Just as Knightley declares that the absence of speech can express love as strongly as its presence, perhaps we are to imagine that Emma's emotion is proportional to the degree to which we actually hear her speak. Social codes often thwart perfect sincerity in speech, but sincere feelings are a remedy to this problem.

CHAPTERS 52–55

SUMMARY: CHAPTER 52

Harriet agrees to Emma's plan to send her to London on the pretense that she needs to see a dentist, which satisfies Emma since she does not want to hurt Harriet with news of Emma and Mr. Knightley's engagement. Emma decides not to tell her father of her engagement until Mrs. Weston, who is pregnant, has given birth to her baby. Meanwhile, she pays a visit to Jane. They are unable to speak openly because Mrs. Elton is there, and Jane's engagement is still supposed to be a secret. However, Emma interprets some of Mrs. Elton's remarks and expressions as ostentatious indications that Mrs. Elton is in on the secret of Jane and Frank's engagement.

Mr. Elton turns up, annoyed that Mr. Knightley has missed a meeting with him. Emma decides he must be waiting for her at Hartfield and leaves. When Jane walks her out, they are reconciled, each feeling that she owes the other an apology, both full of goodwill.

SUMMARY: CHAPTER 53

Mrs. Weston safely delivers a baby girl, much to Emma's delight. Mr. Knightley reminisces about how headstrong Emma was when she was a child. She expresses gratitude that he so often corrected her mistakes, and he asserts that she would have done just as well without him. Emma is grieved that she cannot speak more openly with him about Harriet. Mr. John Knightley congratulates Mr. Knightley and Emma on their engagement, and shocks the couple by saying that he is not surprised by their news.

Emma works up the courage to give her father the news. Mr. Woodhouse is shocked, but he gradually begins to resign himself to it. Mrs. Weston helps persuade him that his happiness will be increased rather than diminished. She is surprised and overwhelmingly pleased by the match. Mr. Weston shares the news with Jane and Miss Bates, and soon Emma and Knightley's engagement is the talk of Highbury. Only the Eltons are displeased that Emma has made such a good match.

SUMMARY: CHAPTER 54

Mr. Knightley has news for Emma: Harriet is to marry Robert Martin. Knightley had sent Mr. Martin to London with a package for his brother while Harriet was there, and Mr. Martin began to spend time with the family. Knightley worries that Emma is upset, but in fact she is thrilled, amazed, and amused at Harriet's rapid recovery. Emma is thankful that she has not done Harriet greater injury, and she is glad that soon she will no longer need to conceal Harriet's emotional state from Knightley.

Emma and Mr. Knightley go to visit Randalls and find Frank and Jane there. At first, Emma's meeting with Frank is awkward, but soon they are back on easy terms, joking about all that has passed. Frank's ability to speak lightly of all he and Jane have suffered is not entirely approved by his fiancée, and Emma feels Knightley's superiority to Frank.

SUMMARY: CHAPTER 55

Harriet returns from London, and Emma is glad to see how completely she has recovered from her infatuation with Knightley. It is revealed that Harriet's father is a tradesman, a respectable person, but not the aristocrat that Emma had predicted. Emma receives Mr. Martin at Hartfield, but realizes that her friendship with Harriet must "change into a calmer sort of good-will" because of their different social positions.

Harriet and Mr. Martin are the first of the newly engaged couples to marry (in September); Frank and Jane will be the last (in November). Jane is visiting the Campbells, and she and Frank will live at Enscombe. Emma would like to be married in October, but it seems Mr. Woodhouse will never agree. But when Mrs. Weston's poultry-house is robbed, Mr. Woodhouse is eager to have Mr. Knightley in the household for protection. The wedding is too modest to please Mrs. Elton, but "the wishes, the hopes, the confidence, the predictions of the small band of true friends who witnessed the ceremony, were fully answered in the perfect happiness of the union."

ANALYSIS: CHAPTERS 52–55

Although *Emma* ends in the traditional manner of a comedy, with a series of weddings to secure everyone's happiness and reaffirm social ties, the question of whether or not the novel's ending is truly happy is often posed. Some critics suggest that Emma regresses, rather than develops, at the end of the novel because she exchanges her independence, energy, and wit for a wish "to grow more worthy of him, whose intentions and judgments had been ever so superior to her own . . . that the lessons of her past folly might teach her humility and circumspection in future." Instead of marrying a man who is her equal, Emma marries a father figure, and, not only will she not be traveling beyond Highbury, she will not even leave her own father's home. Emma's and Mr. Knightley's reminiscences about her childhood remind us that his main role in her life has been as an authority figure and underline the fact that a large portion of her love for him is as someone who can be depended upon to guide her. She is so used to calling him "Mr. Knightley" that she says she will only call him "George" on their wedding day. Emma's position at the end of the novel is strikingly similar to the position she was in at the beginning.

Also, Emma's thoughts about Harriet indicate that Emma has grown more selfish. She takes for granted that their differing social positions mean that they must give up their intimacy. She does not seem to regret her decision or miss Harriet, suggesting that the need to adhere to social conventions overwhelms the affection that she has for Harriet. Emma's thoughts following the revelation of Harriet's parentage demonstrate that class distinctions have value for Emma apart from their association with personal virtue:

> Such was the blood of gentility which Emma had formerly been so ready to vouch for! It was likely to be as untainted, perhaps, as the blood of many a gentleman: but what a connection had she been preparing for Mr. Knightley, or for the Churchills, or even for Mr. Elton! The stain of illegitimacy, unbleached by nobility or wealth, would have been a stain indeed.

In other words, a match between a gentleman and the illegitimate daughter of a tradesperson would be a true contamination. Although at some points the novel seems to entertain the idea that class distinctions might be unfair or unfortunate, ultimately the novel is decidedly conservative. Austen demonstrates that the happiness of a marriage depends upon the couple's being appropriately matched, rather than one of the parties trying to rise above his or her class background.

IMPORTANT QUOTATIONS EXPLAINED

1. The real evils, indeed, of Emma's situation were the power of having rather too much her own way, and a disposition to think a little too well of herself: these were the disadvantages which threatened alloy to her many enjoyments. The danger, however, was at present so unperceived, that they did not by any means rank as misfortunes with her.

This quotation, which appears early in the novel's first chapter, foreshadows the novel's structure as a whole. What Emma fails to perceive—that it is possible to have too much of one's own way or to be too satisfied with oneself—is exactly what she learns over the course of the book. She is permitted too much influence over Harriet and comes to understand that this power threatens not only Harriet's happiness but also her own. Her flirtations with Frank Churchill satisfy her vanity, but they also expose her to embarrassment and hurt and mislead Mr. Knightley.

This quotation also displays Austen's gift for understatement. The narrator's commentary on Emma seems merely part of a standard character introduction. Like so many of the statements in the book, we can only feel the full force of the narrator's observation upon a second reading.

2. The first error, and the worst, lay at her door. It was foolish, it was wrong, to take so active a part in bringing any two people together. It was adventuring too far, assuming too much, making light of what ought to be serious—a trick of what ought to be simple. She was quite concerned and ashamed, and resolved to do such things no more.

These are Emma's reflections after Mr. Elton proposes in Chapter 16, revealing to her that she was wrong in thinking him attached to Harriet. Though Emma is never totally cured of her impulse to make matches for others, here she rightly diagnoses what is wrong with her matchmaking. Courtship should be serious and simple; it should flow naturally from spontaneous affinities and affection between two people. In the novel, courtship rarely follows these guidelines. Mr. Elton's courtship of Emma is marked by the artificiality and ostentation of his compliments, which reveal his underlying lack of real feeling for her. Frank and Emma's flirtation is light and elaborate in its wit, again signaling us that they are not truly meant for each other. At the end of the novel, Mr. Knightley's direct and simple proposal embodies the ideal proposed here.

3. She was vexed beyond what could have been expressed— almost beyond what she could conceal. Never had she felt so agitated, so mortified, grieved, at any circumstance in her life. She was most forcibly struck. The truth of his representation there was no denying. She felt it at her heart. How could she have been so brutal, so cruel to Miss Bates! How could she have exposed herself to such ill opinion in any one she valued! And how suffer him to leave her without saying one word of gratitude, of concurrence, of common kindness!

This quotation comes at the end of Chapter 43. After being reprimanded by Mr. Knightley for insulting Miss Bates at the Box Hill picnic, a deluge of remorse comes over Emma as she realizes the cruelty of her behavior. This quotation marks the point at which Emma's growing self-understanding, which helps her feel how wrongly she has treated Miss Bates, coincides with her growing attachment to Knightley. Her increasing self-knowledge is thus weighted, because it will bring her to or separate her from true love. This moment is also Emma's most emotional in the novel, and it is narrated directly, unlike Mr. Elton's proposal and Emma's response to Mr. Knightley's proposal. That the narrative so directly accesses Emma's remorse underscores its seriousness—it is as if her thoughts have overpowered the narrator's ability to relate them.

4. Emma's eyes were instantly withdrawn; and she sat silently meditating, in a fixed attitude, for a few minutes. A few minutes were sufficient for making her acquainted with her own heart. A mind like hers, once opening to suspicion, made rapid progress; she touched, she admitted, she acknowledged the whole truth. Why was it so much worse that Harriet should be in love with Mr. Knightley than with Frank Churchill? Why was the evil so dreadfully increased

by Harriet's having some hope of a return? It darted through her with the speed of an arrow that Mr. Knightley must marry no one but herself!

This quotation, from Chapter 47, comes in the midst of Emma's conversation with Harriet in which Harriet confesses her feelings for Mr. Knightley. For the majority of the novel, Emma's suspicions and her attention have been misdirected, focusing on Harriet's possible matches and on her speculations about Jane. Once her perceptiveness and ability to see beyond appearances are finally directed appropriately (after her realization that Frank and Jane are engaged), she makes a swift leap forward in her own self-understanding. However, Emma does not come to the realization that she loves Knightley on her own; only her jealousy of Harriet brings her there. The relationship between Emma and Knightley, though based on their private history together, takes shape only in the context of the surrounding web of social relationships.

5.   Seldom, very seldom does complete truth belong to any human disclosure; seldom can it happen that something is not a little disguised, or a little mistaken; but where, as in this case, though the conduct is mistaken, the feelings are not, it may not be very material.

This quotation, which follows Emma and Mr. Knightley's betrothal in Chapter 49, could be taken as the novel's motto. The quotation says that although almost all human speech holds something back, or doesn't tell the entire truth, as long as the speech is loyal to the speaker's feelings, the fact that we talk without complete truth is not a big deal. The novel is filled with disguises and mistakes. Some are more reprehensible than others, and some are more avoidable than others. Though Elton's insincerity and Frank's conscious deception are critically portrayed—and Emma's mistakes gently corrected—we are left with the sense that, to some degree, misunderstandings are made inevitable by the social conventions that govern human intercourse, and by the imperfections of human communication itself. The remedy for such imperfect communication, according to this quotation, is the genuine emotion of the human heart.

KEY FACTS

FULL TITLE
Emma

AUTHOR
Jane Austen

TYPE OF WORK
Novel

GENRE
Comedy of manners

LANGUAGE
English

TIME AND PLACE WRITTEN
1814–1815, Chawton, England

DATE OF FIRST PUBLICATION
1816

PUBLISHER
John Murray

NARRATOR
The narrator is anonymous and narrates some time after the events of the novel take place. The novel is narrated using free indirect discourse, which means that the narrator steps into and out of Emma's thoughts, sometimes using language we would imagine Emma to use without placing it in quotation marks.

POINT OF VIEW
The novel is narrated in the third person by a narrator who tells us what individual characters think and feel, and who also provides insight and commentary. For the most part, the narrator relates events from Emma's perspective, but at times she enters into the thoughts of other characters. Chapter 41, for example, is narrated from Mr. Knightley's perspective.

TONE
Ironic, satirical, sympathetic

TENSE
> Immediate past

SETTING (TIME)
> Early nineteenth century

SETTING (PLACE)
> Highbury, England

PROTAGONIST
> Emma Woodhouse

MAJOR CONFLICT
> Emma struggles to shed her vanity and her fear of confronting her own feelings, both of which cause her to misunderstand those around her and to meddle harmfully in the lives of others.

RISING ACTION
> Emma realizes that she was horribly wrong to think she could make a match between Mr. Elton and Harriet, because not only are the two ill-suited to one another, but Mr. Elton has had feelings for her all along that she intentionally or unintentionally failed to acknowledge. She decides to be in love with Frank and flirts aggressively with him, though she recognizes that her feelings are not, in fact, very strong. When she cruelly insults Miss Bates at the Box Hill party, Mr. Knightley reprimands her, and Emma feels extreme remorse about the cruelty of her actions.

CLIMAX
> Emma realizes that she is in love with Mr. Knightley after Harriet discloses the same to Emma.

FALLING ACTION
> Emma and Mr. Knightley confess their feelings for one another. Knightley proposes to Emma; the happiness of Harriet, Frank, and Jane, which Emma's intrusion had endangered, is secured as Harriet accepts Mr. Martin's proposal and Jane and Frank prepare to marry.

THEMES
> Marriage and social status, the confined nature of women's existence, the blinding power of imagination, the obstacles to open expression

KEY FACTS

MOTIFS
Visits, parties, conversational subtexts

SYMBOLS
The riddle, the word game, tokens of affection

FORESHADOWING
Almost every chapter includes foreshadowing. For example, in
Chapter 27, we are told that Emma "felt as if the spring would
not pass without bringing a crisis, an event, a something to alter
her present composed and tranquil state."

STUDY QUESTIONS &
ESSAY TOPICS

STUDY QUESTIONS

1. *Emma experiences several major revelations in the novel that fundamentally change her understanding of herself and those around her. Which revelation do you think is most important to Emma's development, and why?*

One way to answer this question would be to recognize that Emma undergoes her most decisive transformation when Mr. Elton proposes to her. At this point, she realizes that she has been completely misguided in her interpretation of Elton's behavior, and she also realizes that she herself is implicated in the courtship games that she believed she was manipulating from the sidelines. Another possible answer would focus on Emma's revelation when Mr. Knightley reprimands her after she has insulted Miss Bates. At this moment, Emma understands that her vain pleasure in Frank's flirtations and her sense of superiority to others in the community have been wrong. She also realizes how much Knightley's opinion means to her. One might also argue that Emma's decisive transformation takes place when she realizes that she loves Knightley, or when she agrees to marry him. A successful answer would consider the intensity of Austen's language together with plot developments. For example, the episode in which Knightley reprimands Emma for insulting Miss Bates seems relatively unimportant in terms of the plot, but this scene includes some of the most emotional and dramatic language in the book.

2. *In what ways, if at all, might Emma be considered a feminist novel?*

Emma may be considered a feminist novel because it focuses upon the struggles and development of a strong, intelligent woman. Though Emma's activities—visits, parties, courtship, and marriage—are limited to the traditional sphere, the novel implicitly critiques these limitations, and implies that Emma deserves a wider stage on which to exercise her powers. Furthermore, the novel criticizes the fact that women must be financially dependent by sympathetically depicting the vulnerability of Jane and Miss Bates.

Alternatively, the novel could be considered antifeminist because it seems to suggest that Emma reaches the pinnacle of her development when she accepts the corrections of a man, Mr. Knightley. Not only does Emma give up her former vow of celibate independence, but she marries an older man who is a father figure.

3.   *Frank Churchill and Mr. Knightley represent two different sets of values and two different understandings of manhood. Describe the values that each character represents, and explain how the novel judges these values.*

Frank Churchill is seen by many of the characters as an ideal man because of his good looks, warmth, and charm. He focuses most of his attention on determining what will please each person, and he makes his compliments with wit and style. However, the novel demonstrates that Frank is also flighty, unstable, and able to put his own wishes above social and moral propriety. Mr. Knightley, conversely, is Frank's opposite in many ways. Though also polite and affectionate with those he cares for, Knightley is dignified and reserved. When he expresses an opinion, it is always the correct one and is stated with simplicity and firmness. The novel clearly values Knightley's qualities above Frank's. But the fact that Frank is forgiven at the end and rewarded with the love of a superior woman suggests that the book cannot entirely renounce its infatuation with Frank's charms.

SUGGESTED ESSAY TOPICS

1.   *To what extent does the narrator express approval of Emma, and to what extent does the narrator criticize her? Choose a passage from the novel and analyze the sympathy and/*

or ironic judgment the narrator expresses in relation to
the protagonist.

2. *Emma* is filled with dialogue in which characters
misunderstand each other. Choose a scene from the novel and
describe the mixture of knowledge and ignorance that each
character possesses, and how their situations influence the
way they interpret each other's statements. To what extent are
we positioned to correct the misunderstanding, and to what
extent do we share the misunderstanding until we have more
information?

3. How does humor work in the novel? Select a speech made by
Mr. Woodhouse, Miss Bates, or Mrs. Elton and describe the
techniques Austen uses to make these characters look foolish.
What contradictions, hypocrisies, or absurdities are put in
their mouths? To what extent do we judge these characters
negatively when we see that they are laughable?

4. *Emma* both questions and upholds traditional class
distinctions. What message do you think the novel ultimately
conveys about class?

5. *Emma* is clever but continually mistaken, kindhearted but
capable of callous behavior. Austen commented that Emma is
a heroine "no one but myself will much like." Do you find
Emma likable? Why or why not?

Review & Resources

Quiz

1. What is the name of Mr. Knightley's estate?

    A. Hartfield
    B. Maple Grove
    C. Donwell Abbey
    D. Brunswick Square

2. Which of the following men does Harriet NOT fall in love with?

    A. Mr. Elton
    B. Mr. Weston
    C. Mr. Martin
    D. Mr. Knightley

3. Whose wedding has just taken place when the novel begins?

    A. The Knightleys'
    B. The Eltons'
    C. The Sucklings'
    D. The Westons'

4. What is Jane Fairfax's connection to Miss Bates?

    A. Jane is Miss Bates's sister.
    B. Jane is Miss Bates's niece.
    C. Jane is Miss Bates's childhood friend.
    D. Jane is Miss Bates's mother-in-law.

5. Where did Mr. and Mrs. Elton meet?

    A. In Bath
    B. In Bristol
    C. In Highbury
    D. In London

6. Why does Emma tell Harriet not to marry Mr. Martin?

    A. Emma is in love with Mr. Martin.
    B. Emma thinks Harriet is socially above Mr. Martin.
    C. Emma thinks Mr. Martin is insincere.
    D. Emma thinks Mr. Martin is a scoundrel.

7. Regarding personality, whom does Isabella most resemble?

    A. Emma
    B. Mr. Weston
    C. Mrs. Weston
    D. Her father

8. What was the first Mrs. Weston's maiden name?

    A. Campbell
    B. Churchill
    C. Taylor
    D. Woodhouse

9. What will be Jane's profession if she doesn't marry?

    A. Secretary
    B. Nurse
    C. Governess
    D. Housemaid

10. Why does Frank flirt with Emma?

    A. He wants to marry her.
    B. He wants to conceal his preference for another.
    C. He wants to conceal the fact that he is gay.
    D. He's bored.

11. From whom does Frank rescue Harriet?

    A. Gypsies
    B. A rapist
    C. Robert Martin
    D. Mrs. Elton

12. Who provides for Jane Fairfax's education?

    A. Mrs. Bates
    B. Frank Churchill
    C. Mr. Knightley
    D. Colonel Campbell

13. Which of the couples who get engaged at the end of the novel is the first to get married?

    A. Frank and Jane
    B. Emma and Knightley
    C. Harriet and Mr. Martin
    D. Mr. Woodhouse and Miss Bates

14. Who gives birth to a baby girl?

    A. Isabella
    B. Emma
    C. Mrs. Weston
    D. Mrs. Elton

15. Who owns the property where the Martins live?

    A. Mr. Knightley
    B. Mr. Woodhouse
    C. Mr. Weston
    D. Mr. John Knightley

16. What is the name of the estate where Emma lives?

    A. Abbey-Mills Farm
    B. The vicarage
    C. Donwell Abbey
    D. Hartfield

17. Who first suspects that Frank and Jane have a secret attachment?

    A. Emma
    B. Mrs. Weston
    C. Mr. Knightley
    D. Miss Bates

18. What is the second Mrs. Weston's relationship to Frank?

    A. She is his stepmother.
    B. She is his mother-in-law.
    C. She is his aunt.
    D. She is his former governess.

19. What is the name of the man Mr. Woodhouse relies on for medical advice?

    A. Mr. Wingfield
    B. Mr. Suckling
    C. Mr. Perry
    D. Mr. Cole

20. Where does the ball take place?

    A. The Crown Inn
    B. Randalls
    C. The Legion Club
    D. Hartfield

21. How many proposals does Emma receive over the course of the novel?

    A. Three
    B. None
    C. One
    D. Two

22. Where is Emma's mother?

    A. In Bath for her health.
    B. She died long ago.
    C. She has left Mr. Woodhouse.
    D. Visiting her sister.

23. For whom does Emma believe Harriet has fallen after she gets over Mr. Elton?

    A. Mr. Knightley
    B. Mr. Cox
    C. Frank Churchill
    D. Mr. Coles

24. Who insults Miss Bates at the Box Hill picnic?

   A.   Mrs. Elton
   B.   Harriet
   C.   Emma
   D.   Mr. Weston

25. Who does Mrs. Weston initially think has feelings for Jane?

   A.   Frank Churchill
   B.   Emma
   C.   Mr. Weston
   D.   Mr. Knightley

ANSWER KEY:

1: C; 2: B; 3: D; 4: B; 5: A; 6: B; 7: D; 8: B; 9: C; 10: B;
11: A; 12: D; 13: C; 14: C; 15: C; 16: D; 17: C; 18: A; 19: C;
20: A; 21: D; 22: B; 23: C; 24: C; 25: D

SUGGESTIONS FOR FURTHER READING

BLOOM, HAROLD, ed. *Jane Austen.* New York: Chelsea House, 1986.

BOOTH, WAYNE. *The Rhetoric of Fiction.* New York: Penguin, 1991.

BURROWS, J. F. *Jane Austen's* EMMA. Sydney, Australia: Sydney University Press, 1968.

COOKSON, LINDA, and BRYAN LOUGHREY, eds. *Critical Essays on* EMMA. Harlow, England: Longman, 1988.

COPELAND, EDWARD, and JULIET MCMASTER, eds. *Cambridge Companion to Jane Austen.* New York: Cambridge University Press, 1997.

GILLIE, CHRISTOPHER. *A Preface to Jane Austen.* New York: Longman, 1974.

LODGE, DAVID, ed. *Jane Austen's* EMMA, *A Casebook.* London: Macmillan, 1991.

SparkNotes
Test Preparation
Guides

The SparkNotes team figured it was time to cut standardized tests
down to size. We've studied the tests for you, so that SparkNotes
test prep guides are:

Smarter

Packed with critical-thinking skills and test-
taking strategies that will improve your score.

Better

Fully up to date, covering all new features of the tests,
with study tips on every type of question.

Faster

Our books cover exactly what you need to
know for the test. No more, no less.

SparkNotes™ Literature Guides